W9-BXQ-048

· THEODOR ·
HERZL

· THEODOR ·
HERZL

NORMAN H. FINKELSTEIN

AN IMPACT BIOGRAPHY
FRANKLIN WATTS
NEW YORK LONDON TORONTO SYDNEY
1987

Grateful acknowledgment is made to the following
for permission to quote from copyrighted material.

Doubleday and Company, Inc., for quotations from
The Diaries of Theodor Herzl, edited by Marvin Lowenthal,
Copyright 1956 by Dial Press.
Herzl Press for quotations from The Complete Diaries of
Theodor Herzl, edited by Raphael Patai, Copyright 1970.
Holt, Rinehart and Winston, Inc., for quotations
from Herzl by Amos Elon, Copyright 1975.
Houghton Mifflin and Company, Inc., for quotations from
The Dreyfus Affair: A National Scandal by Betty Schechter,
Copyright 1965 by Betty Jane Schechter.

Library of Congress Cataloging-in-Publication Data

Finkelstein, Norman H.
Theodor Herzl.

(An Impact biography)
Bibliography: p.
Includes index.
Summary: Examines the life of the Austrian journalist
who became the founder of the modern Zionist movement.
1. Herzl, Theodor, 1860-1904—Juvenile literature.
2. Zionists—Austria—Biography—Juvenile literature.
[1. Herzl, Theodor, 1860-1904.   2. Zionists]   I. Title.
DS151.H4F46   1987   956.94'001'0924   [B]   [92]   87-8214
ISBN 0-531-10421-4

FOR ROSALIND

CONTENTS

· THEODOR ·
HERZL

By the rivers of Babylon, there we sat down:
Yea, we wept, when we remembered Zion.
By the river of Basel we sat down,
resolved to weep no more . . .

Israel Zangwill

August 17, 1949. The modern State of Israel was little more than a year old. Quietly and respectfully, thousands lined the road between Tel Aviv and Jerusalem as the funeral procession passed. Along the route a sea of blue-and-white flags fluttered. The people appeared solemn but they were not mournful, because this event marked not the end of a man's life work but the beginning.

Theodor Herzl died in 1904. Forty-five years later, he was being reburied with all the honors due a country's founding father. Visitors from around the world had reserved every available hotel room in Jerusalem while the overflow slept on army cots in hastily opened schools and public buildings. In spite of the enormous crowds, the police did not receive even one single criminal complaint. Twenty thousand people filed by the coffin to pay their last respects.

Although Herzl did not live to witness the founding of the State of Israel on May 14, 1948, he had not only predicted it but fifty years earlier and personally laid the groundwork for its establishment. Yet even he could not have anticipated just how difficult that beginning was to be.

With the end of World War II just three years earlier, Jewish survivors of the Holocaust, by the tens of thousands, had made their way into Palestine. The newcomers had to be housed, clothed, and absorbed into a new society whose economy was in a state of chaos. To make matters worse, the combined armies of Egypt, Lebanon, Syria, Jordan, and Iraq had declared war on Israel on the day after the new Jewish state was proclaimed. The largely rag-tag and ill-equipped Israeli army was dramatically cast into a life-and-death struggle against enemies whose aim was the destruction of the fledgling Jewish country before it could begin functioning. In the battles that followed, 6,000 Israelis died but the young country survived. On July 2, 1949, the last of a series of armistice agreements was signed which put at least a temporary end to the hostilities.

Less than a month after that last armistice, in the luxury of a peaceful moment, a grateful nation took time to participate in this special tribute to Theodor Herzl. As the funeral procession slowly wound its way up the hills to Jerusalem, it made two stops. The first was near the agricultural community of Mikveh Israel where Herzl, on his only visit to the Holy Land, had met with Kaiser Wilhelm II of Germany in 1898. That meeting was only one of many that Herzl had with European rulers and politicians to gain world recognition for this land as the national home for the Jewish people. The second stop was at the town of Rishon L'Zion where Herzl had also visited. There were large crowds at both places. As the funeral procession came into view, huge banners were raised on which were written in Hebrew the prophetic words from Herzl's diary, "When we arrive, Jerusalem will be the most beautiful city in the world."[1]

Herzl's final resting place was on a hillside in Jerusalem which now bears his name, Mount Herzl. As the coffin was slowly lowered into the ground, bags of soil from each of the Jewish settlements and villages in Israel were added to the soil of Jerusalem. Theodor Herzl had come home at last to a free and independent Jewish state.

A day earlier, David Ben-Gurion, Israel's first Prime Minister, placed the importance of Herzl's homecoming in dramatic perspective. "Only two men were privileged to have their remains returned to Israel in the course of 3,300 years . . . both were sons of Jacob. The first was Joseph, who left a testament asking that his remains be returned to Israel with the exodus of the Jews from Egypt, and the second was Herzl."[2]

The concept of a Jewish homeland did not begin with Theodor Herzl. Nor was Herzl the first Jew to feel a special attachment to Israel. Since Biblical times there had been an unbroken connection between the Jewish people and the land they called Eretz Yisroel—the Land of Israel. Whether it was known as Canaan, Israel, Palestine, or the Holy Land, this piece of earth had an importance to Jews that was not only historical but was also religious and emotional. Even when physically separated from that land for short or long periods, Jews never allowed themselves to forget their homeland. Each Passover, no matter where they were living, Jews have concluded their Seder meals with these heartfelt words, "Next year in Jerusalem!"

1
IN THE UTTERMOST WEST

My heart is in the East,
But I am in the uttermost West ...

Judah ha-Levi (c. 1075–1142)

Theodor (Tivador) Herzl was born in Budapest, Hungary on May 2, 1860. His parents, Jacob and Jeanette, were typical of the upper-middle-class Jewish families of the time. While they could trace their ancestry back a few generations, anything earlier was pure conjecture. For the Jews of Europe, family residence in the same community for more than a few hundred years was a rarity. It was not that the Jews enjoyed moving: They had no choice.

Since the time when they were driven out of their land by the Romans during the first century, the Jews had been scattered all over the world. In the countries of Europe, religious discrimination forced the Jews to become a people apart, living on European soil but not considered equal to their non-Jewish neighbors.

Beginning with the French Revolution in 1789, a wave of freedom and enlightenment descended upon the people of Europe. For the Jews, this was like an impossible dream come true. The confining spirit of the ghetto was broken and Jews could, for the first time, dream of attaining at least rights of citizenship in the countries where they had lived for so long.

That breath of fresh air did not yet mean total equality. It was difficult to erase centuries of superstition and hatred with the stroke of a pen. But Jews could now enter professions that were previously closed to them. They could attend public schools and gain admission to the universities. Of perhaps greater importance was their right to equal justice, to political activity, and even to serve in their country's army.

The Herzls never denied their Judaism, but neither did they go out of their way to observe it. For the most part they were assimilated Jews, caught up in the wave of liberalism which had drifted into Hungary from Austria and Germany. Their lifestyle reflected the strong desire to be seen and accepted as loyal and participating citizens of the Austro-Hungarian Empire.

Dori, as young Theodor was called, grew up in a warm, supportive family. The Herzls lived in a fine apartment on one of Budapest's most fashionable streets. Next door was the city's imposing main synagogue which, in keeping with the times, was a liberal house of worship. Unlike the traditional synagogues earlier generations of Jews attended, this synagogue reflected the spirit of assimilation that overtook the Herzls and many other Jews of Western Europe. So while they actively participated in all aspects of their country's cultural and professional life, their synagogue, as liberal and modern as it had become, at least gave them some connection to their heritage and religion.

Dori's father, Jacob, was a successful businessman who had begun life in humble surroundings in a small provincial town. A poor but traditional Jewish upbringing is perhaps the best way to describe his childhood. His formal education was minimal. But unlike his two brothers who, caught up in the intensity of assimilation, were converted to Christianity, Jacob never gave up or denied his Judaism.

The main synagogue in Budapest. The house to the left is where Herzl was born and raised.

In his Budapest home, however, the Jewish influence of the small town was supplanted by the sophisticated and cosmopolitan German language and culture much preferred by the upper classes—and by his wife.

Jacob Herzl was a prim and proper man whose formality and public reserve were inherited by his son. But while Dori's dignified bearing came from his father, his driving ambition and self-confidence can be credited to his mother, Jeanette Diamant Herzl. Dori adored and respected his parents and they, in turn, were deeply devoted to him. His mother especially watched over and guided him in an almost overprotective way, but Dori never resented this and relied on both his parents for advice throughout his life.

Jeanette Herzl's family had lived in Hungary for years. Unlike her husband's religiously observant family, Jeanette's family had been assimilated for a long time and was less pronounced in their Jewish beliefs and attachments. One of her brothers had even served as an officer in the Hungarian army. The strong cultural attachment to Germany that Jacob Herzl had adopted with difficulty was the natural environment in which Jeanette Diamant had grown up.

Dori was a bright and talented child who spent most of his time in the company of his mother and his older sister, Pauline. His father was often away on business trips. His sister, in fact, was his closest childhood friend and confidante. Dori was always neatly and elegantly dressed and projected an image of the model child. But the lonely boy was also moody and self-centered. He had few friends. With his mother and sister always nearby, young Dori developed a vivid imagination and often escaped into the world of daydreams and books.

Once, after reading a story about the Messiah, who, according to the Jewish tradition, was destined to save the world, young Dori had a dream in which the Messiah took him in his arms and flew off toward heaven. There young Dori Herzl of Budapest met Moses. The Messiah turned to Moses and called out, "For this child I have prayed!" To Dori, he said, "Go and announce to the Jews that I will soon come and perform great and wondrous deeds for my people and for all mankind!"[3]

But the Herzl family's commitment to the practice of Judaism was largely superficial. On occasion they would attend Friday night services at the synagogue. They also observed the major religious holidays. In spite of the lack of deep religious commitment, the family considered itself among the leading Jews of Budapest. At the age of eight, for example, Dori's father had him initiated into the most prestigious Jewish communal service agency, the *Chevra Kadisha*, or Holy Brotherhood. The group was devoted to the meritorious work of burying the dead and comforting the mourners. Aside from its practical good works, membership denoted a certain standing in the community. Young Dori Herzl's name was ceremoniously added to the list of members. He probably never even attended a meeting! Ironically, his name was dropped from the membership rolls many years later when he had already become a famous Jewish leader. The reason—nonpayment of dues!

Dori's formal schooling began when he was six years old. He was enrolled in the Jewish Elementary School. Although the school was associated with Budapest's Jewish community, religious instruction was not a major part of the curriculum. Yet, years later, at the height of his Zionist activities, he remembered a thrashing he received at the school because he had failed to remember some details of the Exodus of the Jews from Egypt. "Nowadays," he added, "many schoolmasters would like to thrash me because I remember that Exodus only too well!"

In 1870, at the age of ten, Dori was enrolled in the Municipal *Realschule*, or Secondary Modern School. The school curriculum emphasized science rather than history and the classics. His parents had decided on a science career for their son. In part, Dori reinforced this choice by confiding another of his daydreams to his father.

Perhaps the most talked about man of the day was an engineer, Ferdinand de Lesseps, the builder of the Suez Canal. The newspapers were full of stories about him and his wondrous achievement. As the elder Herzl listened in proud rapture, Dori announced his plan for building an equally impressive canal in the Americas, at the isthmus of Panama.

Unfortunately, daydreaming cannot build impressive technological creations. Dori was certainly creative, but not in the sciences. His talents lay in the humanities—literature and writing—and this choice of school proved to be a mistake. For Dori, writing was an outlet for his imagination and emotions. Encouraged by his mother, he worked hard at his compositions and soon became quite a proficient essayist. He was a harsh self-critic and worked for hours writing and rewriting a composition until it suited his high expectations.

He was still the prim and proper boy he had been in his childhood and his closest companion continued to be his sister Pauline. Together they read young Dori's compositions and poetry to their parents and to family friends. Dori even built a small platform in the living room for their performances.

When Dori was fourteen, he founded a small literary society that consisted of himself, Pauline, a cousin, and several of their friends. Dori himself carefully wrote the group's ground rules and was elected president. The society was called *Wir* (We). Under the president's leadership, the activities of *Wir* were conducted in a most formal atmosphere with dignity and order. Naturally, much of the group's time was devoted to the president's own writings. The first meeting took place on February 22, 1874.

Herzl was known as a prim
and proper schoolboy.

The last meeting was held just a few months later on April 26. The group disbanded shortly thereafter. Dori's presidential authority was apparently too much for his friends to bear!

Even though *Wir* broke apart, Dori continued to concentrate on his writing. As a result, his school work suffered. The report cards his mother carefully saved showed poor marks and low interest. Slowly, his parents began to realize that their son was not destined to be a great engineer. They mercifully put an end to Dori's suffering and removed him from school in the middle of the term in February 1875. Years later, Herzl gave a different reason for leaving the *Realschule*.

> *But I soon lost my earlier love for logarithms and trigonometry, for at that time there was an outspoken anti-Semitic tendency at the school. One of our teachers defined the meaning of the word "heathen" by saying, "Among these are idolators, Mohammedans, and Jews!" I had enough of the school and wanted to attend an institution where classics were studied.*[4]

His parents' assimilation did not protect Dori from the petty anti-Semitism that prevailed in Budapest society. But this did not bring him closer to Jewish observance. In May of 1873, Dori became a man according to Jewish tradition. The Herzls invited family and friends to attend his "confirmation," as liberals called the Bar Mitzvah. There is no record of the boy's actual participation in a formal synagogue service, only the reception that took place in the Herzl home.

To prepare Dori for admission to the *gymnasium*, or classical high school, the Herzls engaged tutors. When he enrolled in the Evangelical Gymnasium later that year, Dori was prepared and confident. His first term marks showed a great improvement over his previous grades. He now studied foreign languages including French, Italian, and English. His knowledge of these languages not only opened his eyes to new and exciting literature in their original languages, but proved invaluable to him later in life when he entered the worlds of journalism and diplomacy.

He read literature of all sorts and kept detailed notes on his readings and reactions. Once, after reading a particularly sharp anti-Semitic speech, he wrote in his notebook that the Jews should look for their own country!

His writing, on a variety of subjects, began to occupy more of his time and attention. His mother and sister supported him at every turn. They thought Dori was a brilliant intellectual with a promising future. Unfortunately, his teachers and fellow students saw him in a completely different light. He was arrogant and conceited, and he treated others as inferiors. During his first few weeks in the new school he made friends with another boy his age. The friendship only lasted a short time, with Dori referring to him as a "simpleminded fellow." His teachers were also not impressed with the well-dressed, self-assured boy. At a time when he should have been thinking about the final high school examination and entering the university, his schoolwork showed a serious lack of interest.

Dori showed enthusiasm only in his writing. Perhaps one of the great moments in his life was the appearance of one of his articles in a noted Budapest newspaper. How proud he and his family were to see young Dori Herzl's name in print! But this success only sharpened his arrogance. He was now positive that he was destined to become a great writer. He submitted material to other newspapers. To one editor he submitted an obviously conceited note. This was no way to win friends or influence hard-nosed editors!

His parents were seriously considering a move to Vienna, the Capital of the Austro-Hungarian Empire and cultural center of the Empire's German speaking population. There, Dori could prepare for a career in which the German language and learning were emphasized. Attending the university in Hungary would have meant working in Hungarian, a language not considered sophisticated and worldly enough by the Herzls and other middle-class Hungarians, Jewish and non-Jewish. Their plan to move was to be implemented faster than anyone could have imagined.

On February 7, 1878, Dori's older sister and closest friend, Pauline, died suddenly of typhoid fever at the age of nineteen. Her unexpected death threw the family into total shock. Dori's reaction to his beloved sister's death seemed to border on indifference. While she lay dying, he went to a coffeehouse and played dominoes. When she died he calmly and carefully wrote the obituary notice for the newspapers. Only later, when the full impact of her death hit him, did he show any emotion. But the loss was a deep one to him, regardless of his initial reaction. He kept mementos of hers and made a visit to her grave in Budapest on the anniversary of her death each year until he himself died.

Dori's plans for his own future seem to have been clear. When Rabbi Kohn, the religious leader of the Budapest synagogue, visited the Herzls during the mourning period, he took the lad aside and asked him about his future plans. "I want to become a writer," Dori answered with confidence. The Rabbi shook his head in disapproval and said, "A writer's career is really no sort of a profession."

The three surviving Herzls abandoned their home and friends in Budapest and, within a week after Pauline's funeral, left Hungary forever. Although Dori would return on occasion—including a trip within a few months to take his final high school examination—from this time onward he dropped his Hungarian connections and became totally Viennese: in language, lifestyle and manner. The German language and culture, which in Budapest had centered mainly around his home and family, now enveloped him totally. With the words of Rabbi Kohn still echoing in his ears, the young Herzl entered the University of Vienna Law School in the autumn of 1878. Although his parents still supported Dori's writing ambitions, they also saw the need for him to pursue a "practical" career.

2

A WRITER

I want to become a writer.

Theodor Herzl

In Vienna, young Theodor was no longer just a distant admirer of German culture. He plunged himself headlong into the numerous activities available to a university student in one of Europe's most cosmopolitan cities. He now took his studies seriously even while he continued his interest in writing. But he also was a spirited participant in all aspects of student life.

He joined a pro-German fraternity called Albia, and like the other pillbox hatted members of the fraternity, he went out drinking and gambling with his brothers. The dapper young man made a striking impression upon all who met him: He was elegantly dressed, handsome, witty, and intelligent. He, in turn, always paid special attention to attractive women.

Each fraternity member was known by a heroic nickname. Herzl's was Tancred, a Christian Crusader who had once set out to conquer Jerusalem. Likewise, every brother was expected to engage in the common fraternity sport of dueling. It was the highest indication of noble manhood for a German student to display a dueling scar earned in the heat of battle. Herzl needed private fencing lessons to prepare for his first and only duel with a member of another fraternity. Tancred earned his scar and sign of manhood when he and his opponent both drew blood and left satisfied.

Although Theodor made a few friends at the University, he never really fit into the closely developed friendship of the fraternity. He was still haughty and intolerant of others just as he had been in his childhood. It didn't take long for most of his brothers to develop a dislike for this know-it-all who always seemed to look down on everyone.

Perhaps as an escape, Theodor again turned to reading and writing and spent a great deal of time by himself. Not that this time was wasted. The young thinker and writer had already seen two of his one-act plays published, quite a feat for an unknown student. Yet he was not satisfied with his life. He had high expectations for himself and knew, in his heart, that he was destined for fame. Dejectedly, in spite of what he had accomplished to date, he wrote in his journal in 1882: "Twenty-two years! and damn little achieved . . . I haven't even the smallest success to show, not a thing to be proud of. . . ." To add to his depression he confidently entered a writing contest sponsored by a leading Viennese newspaper. He did not even receive honorable mention.

During his student days in Vienna, Theodor thought of himself as totally Viennese. His Jewishness was not at all in the forefront of his consciousness. Yet the growing anti-Semitism all around him would soon intrude upon his assimilated and privileged life.

Although Jews in the Austro-Hungarian Empire now had full civil rights, anti-Semitism among the citizens was still common. It is difficult to erase centuries of hatred and superstition in just a few years. But now, instead of the Church- and government-approved anti-Jewish feelings of the past, anti-Semitism adopted a new, scientific look. In the modern age of reason and science, anti-Semitism was made to appear "respectable." Pseudoscientific studies "proved" the inferiority of the Jewish race. Throughout Europe books appeared that challenged any rights the Jews had won thus far. Anti-Semitic political parties even won seats in legislative bodies, where their hatred for the Jews was legitimized as part of the democratic process. In Vienna itself, a notorious anti-Semitic politician, Karl Lueger (Loo-Ayger), would be the city's chief political force for years.

Young Herzl's reading was not limited to his course work or the classics. He also read the popular anti-Jewish "scientific" tracts. One such popular work by a leading German scholar, Eugene Dühring, seemed to have had a lasting impact upon the university student. In *The Jewish Question As a Question of Race, Morals and Civilization,* Dühring had argued that all Jews, regardless of their education, wealth, or assimilation, were dangerous to the Christian majority simply because of their Jewish background. There was no way, he declared, that Jews could become the equals of Christians. This hateful idea filled Herzl with uncontrollable anger, and he needed to vent his rage and frustration. Sitting down to his journal, he took pen in hand and, almost without thinking, wrote an embittered attack on Dühring. Alluding to what would later become his major life's work, the flushed student asked himself why the Jews did not just return to the Holy Land and thereby solve the question of anti-Semitism?

Theodor increasingly devoted time to his reading and writing, leaving less time for the affairs of his fraternity. He did write for and help edit Albia's literary magazine,

*Herzl as a law student at
the University of Vienna*

but his relationship with his fraternity brothers remained cool until March 1883 when he severed all connections with the brethren of Albia. The reason was the popular anti-Semitism of the time as displayed in his fraternity following the death of Richard Wagner.

Wagner was the most popular composer of the German world. He was also one of Europe's most vociferous anti-Semites. In 1850, he wrote one of the earliest "scientific" tracts advancing racial theories as justification for hating Jews. His death in 1883 promoted public displays of mourning throughout Germany and Austria. One such meeting was held by the openly anti-Semitic Union of German Students in Vienna. Among the active participants were members of Albia. The next morning when Herzl read an account of the meeting in the newspaper he was both hurt and disgusted, for the most impassioned and fiery speech at the meeting had been delivered by Hermann Bahr, a member of Albia and one of Theodor's closest friends. Theodor decided he could not remain associated with a group that openly discriminated against Jews. He wrote a polite and carefully worded resignation, signing it with his noble fraternity name, Tancred, and submitted it to Albia. His resignation was accepted without protest.

On May 16, 1884, at the age of twenty-four, Theodor Herzl received his doctorate in law. Throughout his university life, he had been more concerned with literature than with law. But now his formal studies were at an end, and the time had finally come to begin making a living at his chosen career. Herzl was almost distraught. He realized that a career in law was not the profession for him. What he really wanted was fame and fortune as a writer. Working within the confining and highly structured world of lawyers and courts could not possibly allow his creative spirit to flourish.

His parents, who had continued their close relationship with him, realized that all was not well with their son. He needed some time for himself away from the pressures of school and career. A relaxing trip would be just the thing, and so Herzl spent the summer of 1884 traveling through Europe. The sights he saw, the people he met, and the emotions he felt, sparked his imagination and his mind. As he traveled, he wrote down his impressions and thoughts and kept improving his writing skills. Although this trip delayed his entering the world of work, it provided him with valuable experiences which would later become the basis for the literary specialty pieces, known as *feuilletons*,[5] for which Herzl would become noted.

On July 31, Dr. Theodor Herzl was admitted to the bar in Vienna as a full-fledged lawyer. Shortly thereafter he accepted a position as a government attorney. Within a year, he was transferred from Vienna to a court in rural Salzburg. There, amid the tranquility of the Austrian countryside, Theodor made a fateful decision. He would leave his legal career. Not that life was unpleasant as a lawyer. He had spent some of his happiest days in beautiful Salzburg. But as he later recounted, there was not much chance of advancement because he was Jewish. His quiet life in Salzburg was also boring and confining. He needed to move on to greater challenges.

In August 1885, barely a year after joining the legal profession, Herzl submitted his resignation. He would never again practice law. His decision may have been based on an initial publishing success that happened a few months earlier. He had submitted a feuilleton in a writing contest run by the same Viennese newspaper that had failed to recognize his talents in 1882. This time, to his delight, he was selected the winner, and the appearance of his article in print helped push him from the legal to the literary world.

But the publication of his first feuilleton did not disguise the fact that he had no steady employment. His ever-watchful parents decided to send Theodor to Berlin, the major center of German literary culture. Perhaps he could establish himself there as a writer. The letters of introduc-

31

tion he carried with him to Berlin did open the doors of important publishing houses, but resulted in no offers. While he was still in Berin, sensational news reached Herzl through the German press. His play, *Tabarin*, had been produced on the New York stage and had been well received by the audience. The young author was surprised and proud; he was beginning to make a name for himself.

He continued writing. In 1886, after completing another play, *Seine Hoheit* (*His Highness*), he set out on a second trip to France. Writing down his observations and impressions during these trips provided him with the relaxation and enjoyment he needed.

When he returned to Berlin that October, he was still unable to convince anyone to publish his new plays but instead was offered a contract to write reviews from Vienna for a Berlin newspaper. Herzl wrote for that paper until the spring of 1887. Then, feeling depressed, he set out on yet another trip to refresh himself. This time he traveled to Italy. Having learned from past experience, he arranged in advance to report on his trip for various newspapers. This trip was a total success. He felt happy and exuberant, and the articles he wrote were well received by the readers. His name was now well known to the readers of many German language newspapers.

On April 15, 1887, he was appointed feuilleton editor of the *Wiener Allgemeine Zeitung,* an important Viennese newspaper. Within a few months, he received the welcome news that *His Highness* would be produced in a Berlin theater. The previously dejected and insecure writer could no longer doubt his talent and success. Within a short time, two more of his plays were produced, and they too were well received.

For all his newfound fame, Theodor Herzl was still a lonely young man. The unusually close relationship between him and his parents would last his entire life; but this was not enough. Because of his own aloof manner and appearance of superiority, he always found it difficult to make friends with people his own age. Tragically, two of the closest friends he ever had died within a year of each other, leaving a lasting mark of sadness on Herzl.

On June 25, 1889, Dr. Theodor Herzl married Julie Naschauer, the eighteen-year-old daughter of a rich industralist. The Herzls and Naschauers may have known each other only casually in Budapest. But in Vienna, young Theodor became a frequent visitor in the Naschauers' home and fell in love with their pretty daughter. The marriage was destined for failure even before the ceremony took place. The haughty, intellectual young man could never find anything in common with Julie, the spoiled, materialistic daughter of a wealthy Jewish family, who, like the Herzls, had come to Vienna from Budapest. But unlike the Herzls, the Naschauers leaned toward French rather than German culture.

The young couple helped seal their future unhappiness by moving into an apartment near the elder Herzls. In later years, even when they moved farther away, Herzl would often steal away to visit alone with his parents, as his mother was not one to avoid mixing into the affairs of the newly married couple.

Married life did not offer Theodor the peace and quiet he needed for his creative work. Even in the early period of his marriage, he often felt the need to leave his wife and home to travel and write, free from domestic pressures. On March 3, 1890, their first child, a girl, was born. She was named Pauline, after the dead sister who always remained in Herzl's thoughts.

In February 1891 Herzl received the news that a dear friend had committed suicide. Julie was then five months pregnant with their second child. The distraught young father reacted as he always did in time of trouble—he went on a long trip, this time to Italy. He returned home in time for the birth of his only son, Hans, on June 10, 1891.

For the next two months, he quietly suffered through

Julie, Herzl's wife, about 1900

the continuing agony of his home life. The marriage was on the brink of divorce. And the death of his friend still disturbed him. Also nagging at him was the feeling that he was not moving ahead in his career. He was not yet the renowned playwright he wanted to be. He set out on his travels again, this time to Southern France and into Spain. His spirits lifted and he sent his observations back to Vienna's leading newspaper, the *Neue Freie Presse*, where his words were eagerly awaited by appreciative readers.

Suddenly, when he least expected it, Herzl's lifelong search for international recognition materialized in the form of a telegram from the *Neue Freie Presse*. Would Dr. Herzl accept the position of Paris correspondent for the paper? In an age before television network news anchors, the most prestigious position a journalist could dream of was that of a newspaper correspondent in one of the major capitals of the world. As Paris correspondent of the most influential German language newspaper, Theodor Herzl would now become one of the world's noticed people. True, he would have to give up his playwriting. His life would have to be more organized; there could be no more spur-of-the-moment trips. On the other hand, the move to Paris might be just the answer to his marital problems. The fashion-conscious Julie would jump at the chance to live in Paris, the city of style and status (and also away from her prying mother-in-law!).

Flushed with excitement, Herzl immediately cabled back his acceptance. He resigned himself to a life of schedules and routines, even suggesting sarcastically that he would now begin wearing galoshes like a timid business-man. He truly believed that he would never again write for the theater.

Without even bothering to return to Vienna, he went directly to Paris, where he proudly registered in the hotel as the Paris correspondent of the *Neue Freie Presse*. Within a short time, Julie and the two children were settled in a large comfortable house, and Theodor plunged himself

Herzl with his three children:
Hans, Pauline, and Trude

into the rarefied world of a Paris correspondent. On May 20, 1893, his third child, another daughter, Trude Margarethe, was born.

Herzl wrote glowing reports to his readers in Vienna about the arts, culture and lifestyle of the French capital. His reports to the *Neue Freie Presse* were extremely popular and were eagerly anticipated by both his editors and readers. Herzl soon found himself totally immersed in his new life. His reputation as a sensitive and polished journalist continued to grow. In his expanding circle of friends and contacts were the country's leading politicians, authors, and artists. He loved every moment of his new life.

━━━━ 3 ━━━━
IT IS NO DREAM

If you will it, it is no dream.

Theodor Herzl

Herzl's growing reputation as a first-class journalist gave him easy access to the gates of French power. The worldly, well-dressed Austrian socialized freely with the most influential leaders of Parisian society. With his wit and intelligence, he was as welcome in the salons of the intellectuals as he was in the unadorned offices of government bureaucrats. The articles he sent back to Vienna showed the same kind of analytical depth and descriptive detail appreciated by readers of his early travel pieces.

In spite of the liberal and sophisticated world that surrounded him, Herzl could not ignore the undercurrent of anti-Semitism that existed all over Europe. In Paris, there were French anti-Semites. Foremost among them was Edouard-Adolphe Drumont. His book, *La France Juive* (*Jewish France*), quickly became one of the most popular books of the entire nineteenth century. The Jews, Drumont wrote, were responsible for all the ills that affected France. Whatever political, economic, or behavioral complaints people could think of, Drumont blamed on the

Jews. The hatred continued in the columns of his anti-Semitic newspaper, and the "news" he printed was devoured by a growing group of followers. They believed, without any doubt, that all Jews were not only evil but were continually plotting to undermine the lives of all "decent" Frenchmen.

Herzl, like other Jews of his time, tried to push these anti-Semitic rantings to the background as he carried on with his daily activities. In his early writings, the problems of the Jews were mentioned only in passing. Gradually, now, he began to focus more on the specific conditions that affected French public behavior and that ultimately led to the blind prejudice against their Jewish neighbors. His observations tended to be intellectual and unemotional and were written in an unbiased manner much as a scientist coldly describes his experiments. Nonetheless, as a Jew, he himself could not escape the unselective prejudice. Once, on a trip to Austria, he had been discussing anti-Semitism with a friend when some passing youths shouted "Dirty Jew!" at him. Herzl knew that the remark was not intended for him personally. After all, the boys did not even know who he was. But it was this kind of automatic prejudice that so angered him and ultimately led him to seek a solution to the so-called "Jewish Problem."

At first, Herzl indulged in fantasies about some dramatic way to put an end to mindless anti-Semitism. Thinking back to his university days, he imagined a series of duels with the foremost anti-Semites of Europe. If he won, it would demonstrate the justice of his cause. If he were killed, he would become a symbolic martyr to the cause of equality. Next, he proposed that all the Jews of Europe should become Christians. By converting, he reasoned, they would no longer be targets for hatred. Although Herzl continued to perform his duties as correspondent, his mind was becoming increasingly preoccupied with thoughts about curing the world of anti-Semitism.

In October 1894, Herzl found himself in the Paris studio of Samuel Friedrich Beer, the noted Austrian sculptor. He had come to pose for a bust that Beer, an assimilated Viennese Jew like himself, was preparing. During the tedious sitting, the two men engaged in a friendly conversation that ultimately turned to the subject of anti-Semitism. Candidly, Herzl and Beer discussed their own experiences as respected members of society and as Jews. Suddenly, Herzl was struck by the obvious. Here they both were, men of art and culture, yet it seemed impossible to separate themselves in the eyes of gentiles from the ghetto and the Jewish stereotype. Herzl forgot his fantasies about duels and religious conversions as he began to realize that anti-Semites made no distinctions among Jews. Whether assimilated, religious, or even converted to Christianity, a Jew remained a Jew forever in the eyes of gentiles. Although they were no longer confined to the traditional ghettos, Herzl saw the Jews of Europe still imprisoned in the inner ghetto that prevented their being accepted as equals.

That was it! Now that he could clearly see the reason for the hatred, he needed to express himself. His light-hearted writing and his newspaper columns would not do. He rushed home and, setting everything else aside, began writing a play. Seventeen days later he had completed a drama entitled *The New Ghetto*. This was, at last, the vehicle through which the entire issue of anti-Semitism could be discussed and ultimately solved. *The New Ghetto* depicted the problems faced by European Jews as they tried to live in dignity among their Christian neighbors. The leading character's emerging pride in his Jewishness perhaps best illustrates what was happening to Theodor Herzl himself. For even in cultured Europe, the Jew could not live in peace until he was finally allowed to break out of the moral and social ghetto in which he had been confined for so many years. He submitted the play immediately to producers with the hope that it would soon be staged.

While he waited for news about his play, an event was taking shape that would shake France to its foundation and lead Theodor Herzl to world prominence.

That event was called the Dreyfus affair.

On October 15, 1894, an officer of the French Army General Staff, Captain Alfred Dreyfus, was arrested and charged with being a spy for Germany. In 1870, the French had lost a war with Germany and with it the province of Alsace-Lorraine. Since then, the French had nursed a strong resentment against Germany and had an almost irrational fear of subversion and espionage. So while the arrest of a supposed German spy, especially an officer of the general staff, was important, it should not have been serious enough to throw France into political turmoil.

The anti-Semitism that Drumont printed in his book and newspaper was only an indication of the widespread anti-Jewish feeling common in France at the time. This deeply rooted hatred and distrust of Jews was firmly ingrained in the hearts and minds of many Frenchmen. So they did not find it difficult to look upon their Jewish neighbors as "outsiders" capable of committing all sorts of treasonable acts against their country.

An example of this kind of irrational hatred was found in the Panama Canal scandal. A company had been formed in France to build a canal through the isthmus of Panama, shortening the trip from the Atlantic to the Pacific oceans. The very idea was sensational. Herzl himself had dreamed of the idea years earlier as a childhood fantasy. Thousands of hardworking Frenchmen invested their life savings into this "can't fail" company with the hope of making huge profits. When the Panama Canal Company suddenly went bankrupt in 1889, all of France was thrown into turmoil.

Although later investigation would show that the entire company was corrupt, Drumont and other anti-Semites raised shrill cries against "wicked Jewish financiers" who took advantage of honest, unsuspecting, and decent Frenchmen. This, of course, was a lie. But to the French, who were conditioned to anti-Semitism, it was undebatable truth.

Yet two factors blew this event totally out of proportion and engaged the entire country in bitter debate for a decade. First, Captain Dreyfus happened to be Jewish, the only Jew on the general staff. Second, and most important, Captain Dreyfus was innocent of all the charges brought against him.

From the beginning it was not the guilt or innocence of one army officer that mattered. For it was not Dreyfus the French Army Captain who would be on trial, but Dreyfus the Jew. And to a large proportion of the general public (and an even larger proportion of French Army officers), Dreyfus' Jewishness was enough to make him guilty without any question. Ironically, Dreyfus and his family were totally assimilated Jews. Except for the accident of birth, there was nothing to connect the loyal Captain to any aspect of Jewish life.

When Drumont ran a special banner headline in his newspaper on November 1, 1894, it was, not surprisingly, received as certain truth. "HIGH TREASON" the headline roared. "ARREST OF A JEWISH OFFICER, CAPTAIN DREYFUS."

Dreyfus was honestly surprised when the court that tried him declared him guilty. But to most Frenchmen his guilt was a foregone conclusion. There could be no doubt, after all, since Dreyfus was Jewish! Even though an honest army officer had determined that the evidence used to convict Dreyfus was false, most of France was convinced. The country was bitterly divided and continued the debate of Dreyfus's guilt or innocence while the hapless prisoner languished in a vermin-infested cell far away on Devil's Island.

The furious debate led to the arrest and trial of another officer, Major Ferdinand Walsin-Esterhazy. Evidence had been discovered that the major, an aristocrat, was the real spy—not Dreyfus. In 1897, Walsin-Esterhazy was brought to trial. The evidence against him was almost overwhelming, yet the trial ended with his acquittal. When he was officially declared innocent, his supporters went wild. They marched through the streets mingling their cheers and applause with the now familiar cries of "Death to the Jews! Death to the Jews!"

The sight of this rampant anti-Semitism drove the famous French writer Emile Zola into action. In a heated rage, he sat down at his desk and wrote all night. The next morning his words appeared in the newspaper, *L'Aurore*. The blazing headline caught the attention of all France and brought the Dreyfus affair to the forefront of all conversation.

"J'ACCUSE!" (I accuse!) The words leaped off the page and struck at the heart of France. Zola accused the French army and government of waging a war of deceit, lies and anti-Semitism. The army knew Dreyfus was innocent, he charged. They were only using Dreyfus to cover up a national scandal. The accusations only infuriated the street mobs more than before. Rioting broke out against Jews throughout France. Even in towns where no Jews lived, there were patriotic demonstrations. Zola himself was arrested and charged with libel, and France was more divided on the Dreyfus issue than ever before.

It would take another four years for Dreyfus to be freed from his life sentence on Devil's Island. During those years, a resolute Dreyfus sat isolated and disbelieving on the barren island. Meanwhile, a worldwide outcry for justice finally led to the long awaited retrial. This second trial, in 1899, was as carefully staged as the first. The amazed world looked on as the charade was played out. In spite of Zola and his other supporters, Dreyfus was again found guilty. A few days later, the president of France granted Dreyfus a pardon. It was not the verdict of innocence Dreyfus deserved, but at least he was now free. It was only in 1906 that the highest court in France, after reviewing all the inconsistencies and lies, finally declared Dreyfus completely innocent of all charges.

When the Dreyfus affair first erupted in 1894, Theodor Herzl and many French Jews thought that the captain might really be guilty. The doctored evidence that was presented in the press was most convincing. That assumption of guilt was, at the time, understandable. But to Herzl, the basic issue on trial was not the guilt or innocence of an individual who happened to be Jewish. The key issue was the blatant anti-Semitism that surfaced as an automatic response.

On January 5, 1895, shortly after the first trial, Herzl, as correspondent of the *Neue Freie Presse*, had stood in the courtyard of the French Military Academy. Near him were other reporters from French and foreign newspapers. Smartly dressed and precisely arranged rows of soldiers stood at attention. Outside the gates was a tightly packed crowd of civilians straining for a glimpse of what was happening within. Alfred Dreyfus was about to be shipped off to serve a life term on Devil's Island. First he would undergo the humiliating public ceremony marking his degradation as a French army officer. Those present would witness, as the army hoped, the final chapter in the Dreyfus story.

At precisely nine o'clock the sound of marching soldiers was heard. The unruly crowd outside the gate pressed forward for a better view. All eyes were fixed on the slight army captain whose erect bearing and carefully arranged uniform betrayed no sign of remorse. A drum roll announced the entrance of Captain Dreyfus who, accompanied by a military escort, was marched forward toward a waiting general. "Alfred Dreyfus, you are unworthy of your uniform. In the name of the French people we degrade you."[6]

The exuberant mob outside the gate kept up a steady barrage of boos and catcalls. Over and over they shouted,

"Death to the Traitor! Death to the Traitor!" Herzl turned to a colleague and asked, "Why are these people so happy?" His fellow reporter turned to Herzl and replied, "They see him not as a human being but as a Jew. Christian compassion ends before it reaches the Jew. It is unjust but we cannot change it. It has always been so and it will be so forever."[7] Herzl was stunned!

At that particular moment the prisoner was being paraded around the courtyard. The jeers and taunts of the mob grew in intensity. As Dreyfus reached the small knot of newspapermen, he turned toward them and shouted bravely, "You will say to the whole of France that I am innocent!" But even the reporters, normally cool and objective, were caught up in the emotional atmosphere of the scene. Losing whatever professional objectivity they should have exhibited, some of them responded with cries of "Coward!" and "Traitor!" and "Dirty Jew!"

The rousing lilt of military music echoed across the courtyard and over the gates as the soldiers marched away. But Herzl was not paying attention to the music. He heard only the repetitive chants of the mob: The rhythmic cadence almost seemed to mesmerize him. Over and over the same hate-filled phrase echoed in his brain. "Death to the Jew!"

It now became very clear to Herzl. He knew what he had to do. The scene he had just witnessed put the Jewish problem he had given so much thought to in proper perspective. Suddenly all the ways he had come up with to solve the problems of the Jews seemed inadequate and ill conceived. There was only one way to save the Jewish people.

There is no nation without a country! . . . [A Jew] he may feel perfectly at home in a strange land but he must know that somewhere in the world there is a country predestined to be his own and that of his family, a country which must permit him to enter, which cannot

44

refuse him. He does not dream of going to his country, he has no desire to do so: but he knows there is a country that is waiting for him, that belongs to him, and to which he belongs. No man can live without this![8]

Without realizing it, Herzl had become a Zionist!

From that moment until the day he died, Theodor Herzl dedicated his entire life to the establishment of a Jewish homeland. He would later describe the fervor and satisfaction of his involvement by saying, "Zionism was the Sabbath of my life."

4

THE SIMPLE ANCIENT MANEUVER

This simple, ancient maneuver is
the exodus from Egypt.

Theodor Herzl

When Herzl wrote his play, *The New Ghetto*, he hoped
it would focus attention on the problems faced by Europe's
Jews. He was an accomplished and talented writer who was
confident that his play could influence public opinion.
When it turned out that no one would produce his play,
he searched for another way to publicize his ideas. He
turned to the rich and influential Jews of Europe. They
would certainly give him the support and money needed
to get a mass movement off the ground.

Baron Maurice de Hirsch, who lived in Paris, was one
of the wealthiest men in the world. While he busied himself with high-level political and economic problems, he
never forgot his people. In particular, he showed great concern for the poverty and suffering of the East European
Jews. Although anti-Semitism existed openly in Western
Europe, it was in Eastern Europe that prejudice and persecution reached new heights of cruelty. Hirsch founded the
Jewish Colonization Association in an attempt to resettle

46

impoverished Jews from Russia in remote farming villages in Argentina. There, with the Baron's financial backing, Jews could learn basic agricultural skills without the continuous threats of violence they faced in Europe. Here, Herzl thought, was just the man who would be able and willing to help him. Hirsch, after all, had demonstrated an understanding for a dramatic solution to the problems faced by many Jews. Herzl knew he must speak with him and involve him in a political effort to secure a homeland for the Jews.

Baron de Hirsch was not an easy man to see. But Herzl had developed somewhat of a name for himself as the respected correspondent of the *Neue Freie Presse*. On June 2, 1895, the Baron received Herzl cordially in response to a written request for an appointment. Both men quickly saw that, although each was committed to helping Jews, their ultimate purposes were worlds apart. "You breed beggars,"[9] Herzl told the old man. Bluntly, he called the Baron's attention to the need for a mass migration of Jewish people, carefully organized and supported by political authorities. The destination needed to be the Promised Land, not another "foreign" country. Charity handouts alone were not enough. "The first task," Herzl lectured, was "to improve the mass character among Jews. . . ."[10]

Baron de Hirsch interrupted; an annoyed look on his face showed his displeasure. "No, no, no!" he cried. "I do not want to raise the general level. All our misfortunes come from the fact that the Jews want to climb too high. We have too much brains. My intention is to restrain the Jews from pushing ahead. They shouldn't make such great progress. All the hatred against us stems from this."[11]

To Herzl, this line of reasoning was wrong. He knew that even if all the Jews were to become farmers, anti-Semitism would not disappear. Also, the settlements Hirsch had begun in Argentina could only support a small number of people and would not make any noticeable difference in the condition of most European Jews. Furthermore, there was a limit to the amount of money one person, even one as wealthy as Hirsch, could be expected to give away.

In short, there was only one answer for Herzl—a mass, political movement by Jews to secure a permanent and legally recognized homeland; a place, as he later envisioned, where

> *we can have hooked noses and black or red beards . . . without being despised for it. Where at last we can live as free men on our own soil . . . Where we can expect the reward of honor for great deeds so that the derisive cry of "Jew!" may become an honorable appellation, like German, Englishman, Frenchman—in short, like that of all civilized peoples.*[12]

Herzl left the baron's home disappointed at not winning the elderly philanthropist's support. Yet he was even more resolved than before to continue his quest. As he made his way through the bustling Paris streets, he was oblivious to the events surrounding him. Deep in thought, he climbed the stairs to his small room in the Hotel Castille.

Even then, Paris in the summer took on the look of a ghost town. Most of the year-round residents went on vacation, leaving the city in the grip of tourists, essential workers, and others who, for one reason or another, could not get away. Since Parliament was still in session, newspaper correspondents were also obliged to remain in the city. Julie and the children had returned to Vienna for the summer and, rather than keep their large home open just for him, Herzl had rented a simple room for the season at the Castille.

Herzl was in a state of nervous confusion. He knew he had to do something but did not know exactly what. In near feverish excitement, he began jotting down his random thoughts and ideas on pieces of scrap paper which began to litter all parts of the room. The next day, still in the grip of this emotional stranglehold, he wrote a letter to Baron de Hirsch. In it he offered a basic plan for the start of a mass emigration of Jews.

On the same day, he began to write a diary which he entitled "The Jewish Question." He would maintain this diary until his death, by which time it had grown to six thick volumes. Little did Herzl realize that his plays and essays would not become his literary legacy. It was his diary, begun in an atmosphere of near frenzy, that would become his most important and lasting literary contribution to the world.

> *I have been pounding away for some time at a work of tremendous magnitude. I don't know even now if I will be able to carry it through. It bears the aspects of a mighty dream. But for days and weeks it has saturated me to the limits of my consciousness; it goes with me everywhere, hovers behind my ordinary talk, peers at me over the shoulders of my funny, little journalistic work, overwhelms and intoxicates me. What will come of it is still too early to say.*[13]

So anguished was Herzl during those early days in June that he both looked and acted possessed. He kept away from all his acquaintances, avoiding any chance encounters by dining alone in cheap, out-of-the-way restaurants. All the while he kept jotting down the torrent of ideas that continuously bombarded him. It seemed as if he were under the total control of some powerful outside force. No matter where he was or what he tried to do, there was no escape. He began to fear that he was going mad!

Herzl sat at the desk in his hotel room completely asborbed in his writing. He later remarked that as he wrote he heard the flutter of eagles' wings over his head. Beneath this frenzied activity there still remained the hope of enlisting the support of influential Jews to his cause. Herzl now decided to approach the Rothschilds, the richest Jewish family in the world. Like Baron de Hirsch, the

Rothschilds had long been involved in establishing and funding Jewish settlements to help the suffering East European Jews. Unlike Hirsch, the Rothschilds had chosen to settle Jews in Palestine. To Herzl, this was a positive indication of their certain commitment to a Jewish homeland. If Hirsch had not been receptive to his idea, the Rothschilds would certainly be!

He collected the scraps of paper strewn about his room and tried to arrange his ideas in some orderly manner. Then, he continued writing. What emerged was a fifty-four page section of his diary which he called "Address to the Rothschilds." In a rambling and sometimes disjointed presentation, Herzl laid out his plans and ideas for establishing a Jewish homeland. From specific thoughts on how the country should handle its public works, immigration, land purchasing, and fundraising to lofty pronouncements on religious and political life, Herzl offered an idealist's view of what the future could hold. As his model, he turned to what he called that "simple ancient maneuver—the exodus from Egypt."

When he had finished his "address," it suddenly dawned on him that he needed some special way to bring it to the attention of the Rothschilds. He found that way. He would ask Moritz Güdemann, the Chief Rabbi of Vienna and an acquaintance of the Rothschilds, for help. He quickly dashed off a letter to the rabbi, a man he had never met. In it he confidently stated that he was taking a leadership role in "an action on behalf of the Jews."

Rabbi Güdemann was invited to join with him. In order to get the plans started, Herzl requested a meeting within a few days. Although he had heard of Herzl, the journalist, by reputation and knew Julie's family in Vienna, the rabbi sent back a polite note declining the invitation. Herzl then sent him a second, more detailed letter in which he boldly stated that although it might sound crazy, he had the solution to the Jewish problem. Herzl then asked if the Rabbi would present his ideas to the Rothschilds.

Just then, after Herzl had mailed the letter, there was a knock at the door. It was a friend and fellow reporter, Dr. Friedrich Schiff. As the door opened, Schiff could not believe what he saw. His friend, usually well dressed and meticulously groomed, looked terrible. His hair was disheveled and his clothes were in disarray. The room was littered with scraps of paper. Herzl welcomed his visitor and with nervous anticipation asked him to listen to what he had written. As the astounded Schiff looked on, Herzl began reading aloud his "Address to the Rothschilds." Schiff was the first person with whom Herzl could share his writing on a face-to-face basis. While he read, he kept glancing at his friend for a reaction. Before long Herzl noticed tears welling up in his friend's eyes. A truly welcome sign! The first person to actually hear his plan was overcome with emotion! Alas, Schiff was shedding tears for another reason: He sincerely believed that his friend, Herzl, had gone insane. Almost speechless, Schiff, who was also a physician, urged his friend to seek psychiatric help.

Herzl could not give up his captive audience and showed Schiff a copy of the letter he had just mailed to Rabbi Güdemann. When Schiff heard the contents of the letter, he could not control himself and cried out that the rabbi would think Herzl ridiculous or tragic for writing such a letter. Furthermore, he might even tell Herzl's parents and they would be devastated. Understanding the value of his friend's words, Herzl quickly sent a telegram to Vienna and retrieved the letter.

The next morning Schiff returned to his friend and urged him to forget his crazy ideas. Otherwise, everyone would think he had completely lost his senses. Schiff was able to calm Herzl down and get him to begin looking objectively at what he had done. But while Herzl was regaining his emotional balance, he wrote two more letters. The first was to his original contact, Baron de Hirsch. "I have given the matter up," he wrote. Yet within a few days, in a second letter, he expressed his views to Prince Otto von Bismarck, the elder statesman of Germany. The Prince never responded.

Within a few days, Herzl regained his composure. Yet he would never really be the same person again. Whatever he would do or wherever he would go, an overwhelming passion for a Jewish homeland remained within him. He returned to work, and to the casual observer nothing seemed amiss. He wrote brilliant articles on parliamentary life in France which were so well received by his newspaper readers they were later published in book form. But being the Paris correspondent of a leading newspaper was a full-time job. Herzl knew he could not continue in that pressure-laden situation for long if he also wanted to work for the Jewish cause. On July 27, 1895, he left Paris and his position as correspondent for the *Neue Freie Presse* and returned to Vienna. "And today I am leaving Paris!" he wrote. "One book of my life is ending. A new one is beginning. Of what kind?"[14]

5

THEY WILL HAVE IT

The Jews who wish for a state will
have it and they will deserve to have it.

Theodor Herzl

Herzl's Jewish consciousness had been awakened in Paris. There he began to understand that the callous anti-Semitism he encountered could be cured in only one way. If the Jews had their own land, like all other nations, they could then lead "normal" lives. With that idea in his mind, he returned to Vienna. The publishers of his paper were truly saddened to lose Herzl as their Paris correspondent: They couldn't understand his action. But rather than lose him completely, they lowered his salary and appointed him as feuilleton editor. His supervisors at the newspaper were all Jewish, yet they never supported his Zionist work. Indeed, the relationship between Herzl and the *Neue Freie Presse* remained strained to the very end. Herzl, on the one hand, needed the newspaper for the salary it provided; the newspaper, on the other hand, couldn't deny Herzl's popularity among its readers. Until the day he died, the paper never mentioned Zionism or Herzl's growing role as a Jewish leader. Even when he had become internationally famous, his own newspaper would print nothing about him or the movement of which he had become the leader.

If Herzl expected to find a less anti-Semitic atmosphere in Vienna than in Paris, he was to be disappointed. In the years since his university days, the anti-Jewish climate in the city had grown tremendously. Even the city council was dominated by avowed anti-Semites. But as he got himself settled in his adopted city, those factors faded into the background. What mattered was the reunion of the Herzl family. Theodor, Julie, and the children were together again. Nearby, the elder Herzels, Jacob and Jeanette, hovered, ready to give their son any assistance he needed.

In spite of the family reunion, the relationship between Theodor and Julie, never a model of domestic bliss, deteriorated. Theodor immersed himself in his Jewish work while balancing his newspaper responsibilities. He began traveling again throughout Europe looking for support for his idea of a Jewish homeland. During the rare periods he was home, there was little time for his family. Soon, visitors of all sorts would make their way to the Herzl home, much to Julie's chagrin.

One of the first meetings Herzl arranged took place in Munich, Germany. There, he finally was able to present his "Address to the Rothschilds" to Rabbi Güdemann. The rabbi was charmed by Herzl and his words and even compared the journalist to Moses. Yet he did not think this address was the best way to reach the Rothschilds. The rabbi advised him to return to Paris instead and contact some people who had similar ideas about a Jewish state. So, in November, with a letter of introduction from Güdemann, Herzl returned to the city he had recently abandoned to meet with the Chief Rabbi of Paris, Zadoc Cohen. Although nothing came of this meeting, two other men Herzl met in Paris would have a lasting impression upon him.

The first was Narcisse Leven, the secretary of the Alli-

Herzl, reunited with his
children and parents

ance Israélite Universelle, a worldwide social service organization. He too did not put much stock in Herzl's address but told him of Zionist societies already in existence in Russia, France, and England. Unlike Herzl's preoccupation with intellectual and reasoned arguments for a Jewish state, these Zionists had a more pressing and practical goal: to provide an immediate avenue of escape for the long suffering European Jews from the daily discrimination, hunger, and poverty that surrounded them. The second, and perhaps most important contact he made, was the noted writer, social thinker, and psychiatrist, Dr. Max Nordau. Herzl had known Nordau when they both lived in Paris. In fact, Nordau was the psychiatrist Schiff had suggested Herzl consult. Nordau listened to Herzl, and when the idea for a Jewish homeland was fully explained, he grabbed the surprised journalist's hand and announced his wholehearted support. Nordau would remain at Herzl's side from that moment on.

Nordau encouraged Herzl to visit England and make contact with the active and influential Zionists there. Up to that point, Herzl thought he was alone in his quest for a Jewish land. This visit to Paris had opened his eyes to the fact that there already existed a small network of Zionist activists scattered through Europe. Gladly, he accepted Nordau's letter of introduction to the noted writer Israel Zangwill and set out for London.

London provided Herzl with the emotional support he needed. Zangwill received Herzl warmly and arranged for him to address the Maccabean Club, a group dedicated to the establishment of a Jewish homeland. Herzl's speech, delivered in heavily accented English, was warmly received by the members. During the visit Herzl met a number of important Zionist leaders including Colonel A. E. Goldsmid, a Jewish officer in the British Army. Herzl was treated like a celebrity and even gave a detailed interview to the English language newspaper, the *Jewish Chronicle*.

Herzl returned to Vienna in an enthusiastic mood.

There were others in the world who shared his vision and had been working hard to organize. Many of these Zionists seemed to be just ordinary people: students, immigrants from Eastern Europe, and workers. As he traveled home it began to dawn upon him that his activities until now had been directed to the wrong quarter. The rich and established Jews had no real interest in a Jewish homeland. They wanted to keep things as they were. Having worked hard to gain equal status in their own countries, they did not want to arouse even a hint of any wrongly perceived disloyalty. No, Herzl must turn his efforts to the common Jews of Europe. But how?

His play, *The New Ghetto*, was still unsold and unproduced. Upon rereading the "Address to the Rothschilds," he found that it seemed stilted, disjointed, and, in parts, even poorly written. The main ideas were still valid, but he was, as a writer, disappointed in his own style. Feeling better than when he created the "Address," he now devoted his efforts to a thorough rewriting. This time, he wrote with a clear mind, using his professional writing skills to best advantage.

While he was rewriting his "Address," a revealing incident occurred which illustrates Herzl's view of his mission. It was Christmas Eve and Herzl, taking a break from his writing, was helping his children light a Christmas tree. Just then, Rabbi Güdemann came to call. As the rabbi entered the room, he could not believe his eyes. Here was the self-proclaimed advocate of the Jews busily engaged in a totally Christian practice. Herzl could not see anything wrong with what he was doing. To him, the tree was only a symbol of the Christmas season and had no religious significance. And above all, the children felt good about having one in the house. His writings also reflected this view. The religious aspect of a return to the Jewish homeland was not his primary concern. He was laying the groundwork for a Jewish land that would be established by human hands and not by an act of God.

57

Jeanette, Herzl's mother,
standing beside him in his study

The work in which he was now so engrossed demonstrated how far removed he was from religious ideology. To most religious Jews, a man-made return to Zion was beyond belief. Only God, through the Messiah who was yet to come, could bring the Jews back to their ancient land. Yet Herzl hardly mentioned these timeless cultural and religious roots. Indeed, the title he chose for his rewritten "Address" clearly demonstrated his thinking: *The Jewish State: An Attempt at a Modern Solution of the Jewish Question.*

Little did Herzl realize the impact this little book would have on the world. Even before its publication date, February 14, 1896, favorable reaction to his ideas had already surfaced. In large measure this was a result of the newspaper accounts of his address to the Maccabean Club in London. Within days of the book's appearance in bookstores, Herzl had become the hero of the Jewish student and Zionist groups of Europe. The message Herzl presented to them was both simple and magnetic. "The idea which I have developed in this pamphlet is a very old one," he wrote in the introduction. "It is the restoration of the Jewish State."

Herzl's colleagues on the newspaper and his own family friends were astonished. Had Herzl lost his mind? How else could his obsession be explained? He was a journalist of note, a cosmopolitan university graduate who mixed easily in important circles. He was no political scientist and certainly no religious fanatic. They could find no reasonable explanation for Herzl's sudden and total preoccupation with this Jewish cause.

But others saw Herzl's work in a more positive light. *The Jewish State* was a call to action. In a poignantly vivid style, Herzl presented an introduction to the plight of European Jews. Then, in clear detail, he laid out the blueprint for solving the problem. As Herzl explained it, the problem was a simple one. The Jews, no matter how assimilated or patriotic, were viewed as strangers. The legal rights they might have gained could not erase the centuries-old tradition of anti-Semitism. The solution? A country of their own. But what about the Jews who did not want a new homeland and preferred to remain in their native lands? They would be able to continue their lives securely knowing that there existed a Jewish homeland that belonged to all Jews. "We are a people," Herzl wrote, "one people." [15]

There was a positiveness and certainty about Herzl's writing that made the idea of a Jewish land seem almost a foregone conclusion. There was no doubt in his mind about the correctness of his idea and its ultimate success. "The Jews who wish for a State shall have it, and they will deserve to have it." [16]

Herzl may have been a dreamer but he was no fool. He knew that the establishment of a Jewish state required the assent and cooperation of the world's most powerful nations. Without this international political support, there could be no success. Also, the Jews themselves now had to organize and lobby for the right to their own land. To that end, Herzl suggested the establishment of three agencies to further the organizational needs of the world's Jews: The Jewish Company, the Society of Jews, and local groups in every country to organize emigration to the homeland.

The Jewish Company would be responsible for practical details related to the creation of a workable society in the new land. The Company would build cities, purchase and lease land, control work assignments, and supervise business.

The Society of Jews would act as the overall political and governmental agency for all Jews. The Society would negotiate the establishment of a Jewish homeland by, in effect, establishing diplomatic relations with the countries of the world.

The third component would be local groups to be set up in each country to assist in the emigration of Jews. Here Herzl assigned an important role to rabbis. They would provide the spiritual help necessary for such a traumatic venture.

The Jewish State then presented a vision of what this new land would look like. Although the practice of religion would be encouraged, the country would not be a theocracy. Since Jews came from a number of countries, multiple languages would be promoted. A seven-hour work day would also be legalized to indicate the concern the country had for its people. But the establishment of a Jewish homeland would have other benefits, not just for the Jews but for the world.

We shall live at last as free men on our own soil and die peacefully in our own homes. The world will be freed by our liberty, enriched by our wealth, magnified by our greatness. And whatever we attempt there to accomplish for our welfare, will react powerfully for the good of humanity.[17]

While he did not realize it at the time, the basic ideas Herzl presented in the pages of *The Jewish State* were not original. In fact, as he sat in Vienna editing and polishing his work, small groups of Jewish settlers were already establishing themselves in Palestine. In Europe, as Herzl himself had seen in England, Zionist organizations dedicated to the same goal had sprung up. But these groups had been working almost unnoticed outside of their own circles. For years they had been meeting, issuing publications, and debating among themselves. They were strongest in Russia, where the first modern Zionist awakening occurred.

Moses Hess, a German Jewish Socialist, had written a pamphlet in 1862 called *Rome and Jerusalem*, in which he argued for the restoration of a Jewish homeland, under the protection of a European power, as the only way to eliminate anti-Semitism. He forcefully stated that the Jews were not only a religious group but a separate nation and, therefore, needed to be returned to Palestine. In response to Hess's arguments, small groups of supporters organized themselves throughout Russia. They called themselves Hovevey Zion (Lovers of Zion). They set two major goals for themselves. The first was to develop organized Jewish immigration to Palestine. The second, which had a more visible relevance to Eastern European Jews, was the revival of the Hebrew language and culture. For centuries, Hebrew as an everyday language had been overtaken by Yiddish as the universal language of Europe's Jews. Classical Hebrew was reserved, by and large, for prayer and religious study.

By 1884, when Herzl had just received his law degree, the scattered branches of the Lovers of Zion had formed a federation. More importantly, they gained the financial support of Baron Edmond de Rothschild. In 1878, with funds supplied by the Baron, they established the settlement of Petach Tikvah in Palestine. This was the second modern Jewish settlement in Palestine and joined Mikveh Israel, which had been in existence since 1870. Both settlements consisted of Russian Jews who were dependent upon charitable contributions for their existence.

It was no accident that this early Zionist activity was largely centered in Russia. For years Russian Jews had been suffering under terrible conditions. Under the rule of the Czars, anti-Semitism was, in large measure, an instrument of government policy. The word "pogrom," used to describe a planned raid on Jews and their property, is of Russian origin. After a particularly devastating series of attacks against Jews in the early 1880s, Russian Jews responded to the pogroms in several ways. A large number saw the hopelessness of the situation and emigrated to safer parts of Europe. This period also marked the start of a major influx of Eastern European Jews into the United States. By the time World War I broke out, millions of Jews from Eastern Europe were beginning new lives amid the opportunities and freedoms of the New World.

Still others became involved in the efforts of the Lovers of Zion. Soon, carried along with the mass Jewish emigration of the time, chapters were founded in the leading Western European countries as well. In Vienna itself, where Herzl was struggling with the ideas for a Jewish homeland, one of these Eastern European activists, Nathan Birnbaum, had coined the name for the movement Herzl was about to lead: "Zionism."

The leader of the Lovers of Zion was a Russian physician, Dr. Leo Pinsker. The pogroms of 1881 had so moved him that he was compelled to write an essay which he called "Auto-Emancipation." Referring to anti-Semitism as a disease, he forcefully proclaimed the cure: a Jewish homeland where all Jews could feel wanted. The writings of Hess and Pinsker inspired the growing number of Jews to action. But there was little they could do. Even among the majority of Jews there was little interest in this utopian dreaming. Outside the closely knit Zionist community few paid any attention to what Hess and Pinsker thought. So when Herzl's *The Jewish State* burst upon the scene, it electrified Zionists. Here was a noted Viennese journalist and playwright bringing the cause for a Jewish homeland to the public all by himself, without any connection to the existing Zionist movement. Ironically, Herzl had never even heard of the two Zionist philosophers, Hess and Pinsker. Years later he would say that had he known of Pinsker's writings he probably would never have written *The Jewish State!*

Theodor Herzl quickly found himself the acclaimed leader of the Zionist cause. From all over Europe he began receiving letters of support. Leaders of Zionist groups made their way to Vienna to meet him, and invitations began arriving urging him to speak to Zionist groups in other countries. He was succeeding where Hess, Pinsker, and others had not succeeded precisely because, unlike them, he was a Westernized, assimilated Jew. He had taken the problem of anti-Semitism beyond the narrow confines of the Zionist world and made its solution dependent as much on international diplomacy as on Jewish self-determination.

Overnight, Herzl's name was heard in Jewish communities all over Europe. To some, he was a prophet, the Moses of modern times. To ultra-Orthodox and Reform Jewish leaders, however, his name did not convey the same magic. To the Orthodox, Herzl's ideas were dangerously close to heresy; they felt only the Messiah himself could bring about a return of the Jews to their ancient homeland. To the Reform, Herzl was nothing but a troublemaker. As full citizens of their native lands, they wanted nothing to do with any separate Jewish country: Only by assimilating could they gain their security.

Nowhere were Herzl's virtues extolled more than in Russia, where conditions had become much worse for the Jews. So when news of Herzl reached the small villages where many of Russia's Jews lived, the response was positive. Even amidst their worst suffering, the Jews, in their prayers and customs, had always kept alive the yearning for their return to Palestine. Invariably, the Jews of these small towns knew more about the geography of the Holy Land than that of their neighboring Russian provinces. They even observed all the religious holidays that dealt with the harvest seasons in that far-off land. Their children, restive in that constrictive environment, actively joined the Zionist ranks to make their parents' dreams come true.

Herzl had been totally ignorant of the Russian Jews and the beginnings of modern Zionism. He wrote *The Jewish State* as his personal manifesto based on his own insight and experience. Now, as the committed Zionists of Europe flocked around him, Herzl began to understand and appreciate their attachment to the cause. He was no longer alone. Indeed, he had unknowingly placed himself at the leadership of what would ultimately become the most successful movement for national liberation in modern times.

6

ONLY ONE WAY OUT

There is only one way out . . .
into the Promised Land.

Theodor Herzl

Herzl's next task was to arrange appointments with the important political leaders of Europe. But even for the noted Viennese journalist, this would not be easy. Suddenly, two unlikely people, both non-Jewish, appeared on the scene. They would provide Herzl with the keys to the chambers of power and elevate him to the position of international diplomat. The first man was an English Protestant minister; the second was a Polish nobleman and sophisticated political agent.

The Reverend William H. Hechler was chaplain at the British Embassy in Vienna. He was a sensitive man whose long gray beard gave him the look of a Biblical prophet. Indeed, he was totally immersed in the world of the Bible and believed that the second coming of Christ was about to occur. That momentous event, he believed, would be preceded by the return of the Jewish people to their homeland in Palestine. When Hechler read Herzl's *The Jewish State,* he immediately offered to help the

Zionist cause. For while Herzl looked upon the cause as a political and nationalistic one, Hechler saw it as a fulfillment of Biblical prophecy.

When Hechler first came to him, Herzl didn't know what to think. Was Hechler crazy or was he serious? It didn't take Herzl long to realize that the man he was talking to was more than a religious zealot. He was a man who might arrange an introduction for Herzl with the ruler of the German Empire, Kaiser Wilhelm II. Hechler, as it turned out, was a former tutor to the children of the Grand Duke of Baden. The Grand Duke, in turn, was the respected uncle of the Kaiser himself.

Hechler offered to attempt the arrangement of an interview for Herzl with the Kaiser. In return, Hechler asked only for the payment of his travel expenses. Herzl, still suspicious of the minister's motives, told Hechler to try.

For over a month Herzl waited for Hechler's response. On April 21, 1896, he heard of the death of Baron de Hirsch. That same day, at last, Herzl received a telegram from Hechler urging him to come to Karlsruhe at once. There he would be received personally by the Kaiser's uncle, the Grand Duke Friedrich of Baden. Herzl, numbed into shock at the death of Hirsch, the rich man in whom he had put so much hope, was now revitalized by Hechler's telegram. Herzl would now gain admission to the exalted company of royalty. On the next day, Herzl boarded the Orient Express in Vienna and made his way to Karlsruhe.

Herzl, the world-class journalist, was nervous. As usual, he had taken great pains to make sure he looked just right. Yet inwardly he felt unsure of himself and was even a little embarrassed. Nervously, he paced up and down in the anteroom of the palace as he waited to be received by the Grand Duke. His friend, Hechler, waited with him, giving him words of encouragement and telling him that the Grand Duke was only a man, just as they were. Suddenly, they were in the presence of the Grand Duke himself. The Duke received Hechler warmly and almost ignored Herzl. But as the conversation continued, the Grand Duke became friendlier toward Herzl. Herzl presented his ideas on the need for a Jewish homeland and eloquently responded to all the Duke's questions. The audience lasted for two and a half hours. Hechler spoke to the Duke in praise of Herzl and his ideas as the fulfillment of prophecy. The Duke was overcome with emotion as he expressed his hope that Herzl's dream would be realized. As they parted, the old Duke warmly grasped Herzl's hand and assured him of his support. He would, the Duke promised, remain in touch. A few weeks later, true to his word, the Duke recommended Herzl to his royal nephew, the Kaiser.

Count Philip Michael de Nevlinski was not a man of God. Yet, like Hechler, he would open the doors of royalty to Herzl. Nevlinski was a shadowy political opera- tive who intimately knew the ins and outs of the Turkish Empire and its politics. Although he was nearly penniless, he led a lavish life by spending the money of those who hired him to represent their interests at the Turkish Court. For Herzl, the Turkish connection was vital to the estab- lishment of a Jewish state. For while Germany was the major European power with influence over Turkey, it was the Turkish Sultan who was the actual ruler of Palestine. Herzl knew that in order for a Jewish state to be founded he would need the support of both countries. Through a Zionist friend, Herzl was introduced to Nevlinski. Although their relationship would be an expensive one for Herzl, the Count was invaluable in leading Herzl through the in- trigues of Turkish politics into the inner sanctum of the Sultan himself.

Although Herzl was deeply involved with Hechler and Nevlinski, he continued to work at pulling together the Zionist organization that had begun to gather around him. Herzl knew that if he was to be considered a real leader he would have to demonstrate his political skills publicly. To this end, an audience with the Sultan of Turkey was a necessity. On June 15, 1896, Herzl again boarded the Orient

Express. This time he was going to the Turkish capital, Constantinople, and Nevlinski was traveling with him.

The train trip provided an opportunity for both men to impress each other. Count de Nevlinski introduced Herzl to several high-ranking Turkish officials who were on board, thus showing how strong his connections were within the Turkish government. Herzl had a chance to show off his connections, too. As the train pulled into the station at Sofia, Bulgaria, a huge, noisy, and exuberant crowd thronged the platform. The people were there to greet Dr. Theodor Herzl and wish him well on his visit to the Sultan. "Long live Herzl! Long live the Jews! Next year in Jerusalem!" the crowd cheered and shouted with enthusiasm. Nevlinski was impressed. To the Turkish officials on board, the scene was a revelation. This passenger from Vienna was a man with a following! And that was exactly the image Herzl wished to create. When he arrived in the Turkish capital, Herzl registered at the finest hotel in the city and was given the royal suite.

Herzl remained in Constantinople for a week and a half. During that time he did not meet the Sultan in person. However, he was received by important officials of the Sultan's Court, including the Grand Vizier. Because of Count de Nevlinski, or perhaps because of his own association with the *Neue Freie Presse,* Herzl found doors open to him that would otherwise have been closed. The message Herzl gave to every official he met was simple: Give us Palestine and the Jews would help Turkey out of her deep financial troubles. In the latter part of the nineteenth century, Turkey was known as the "sick man of Europe." Its image throughout the world was badly damaged not only on account of its money problems, but because of the atrocities the country allegedly committed against its Armenian population.

If the Turks thought that Herzl, the journalist, could solve their problems, they were wrong. If Herzl thought he could pry away some land from the Sultan, he was mistaken, too. For in spite of the crowds of wellwishers at the Sofia railroad station, Herzl, at this point, officially represented no one but himself.

Although he did not meet with Herzl, the Sultan did meet with Nevlinski. Nothing was promised on either side, only that lines of communication would remain open. As a token, the Sultan, through Nevlinski, presented Herzl with an impressive medal of honor, "The Commanders Cross of the Order of the Medjidje."

To the Zionists of Europe, the details of Herzl's trip to Constantinople were of little consequence. The mere fact that Herzl was received by court officials was enough to raise hopes. The Sultan's medal also added to the overall happiness. As Herzl's train stopped in Sofia on the return trip, the crowds who came to greet him were even larger and more enthusiastic than before. This time, Herzl was escorted off the train and led to the main synagogue amid cheers and waving. In an awkward moment, as he stood in front of the Holy Ark, not wishing to turn his back to it in order to face the crowd, a voice was heard from the audience. "It's all right for you to turn your back to the Ark, you are holier than the Torah."[18] People pressed in upon him—some even tried to kiss his hand!

Herzl was a bit surprised and perplexed at all this personal attention. He began to see that the idea of a Jewish state was being accepted with greater enthusiasm by the masses than by the rich Jews. If he needed any more evidence, his next trip to London would provide it.

Herzl's major concern now was money. If he could raise the millions necessary, he imagined that his negotiating position with Turkey would greatly improve. But the millionaires, while polite and understanding, were also protective of their money. Even the devoted members of the Maccabean Club, where Herzl was so gallantly received on his first London visit, were now much colder toward him. They were strong supporters of Zionism as long as it remained a topic for gentlemanly debate. Herzl's public call for political activism made them nervous.

In contrast, the reception Herzl received in London's East End was tumultuous and heartfelt. There, poor Jews who had come from Eastern Europe joyously greeted Herzl as another Moses. Herzl did not disappoint them. With his striking profile and correct manner, he projected a majestic image. His words electrified the audience. "We are a people, one people," he dramatically exclaimed. The crowd cheered and cheered. Even after he sat down, the adulation of the crowd was still quite evident. Its effect upon Herzl was even stronger than he had felt in Sofia. "I saw and heard my legend being born,"[19] he would later write of the experience. Like the Jews in Sofia, the Jews of London's East End believed that Herzl could and would restore them to their ancient homeland. Herzl himself realized that his strength lay not in the money of the rich but in the exuberance and loyalty of the masses.

Herzl now finally got the opportunity to present his "Address to the Rothschilds." On July 18, 1896, Theodor Herzl found himself in the palatial Paris home of Baron Edmond de Rothschild. This man had given a small fortune to establish and maintain Jewish settlements in Palestine. Herzl turned to him and gave him a stern lecture. "You do not know what it is all about. Let me explain it to you first. A colony is a little state; a state is a big colony. You want to build a small state, I a big colony."[20] Their conversation was argumentative, with neither man able to sway the other away from his views. Finally, seeing that nothing more was to be gained by prolonging the conversation, Herzl said in a tone of exasperation, "You are not willing—I have done my share."[21] Both men exchanged pleasantries and Herzl left. As he shut the door behind him, Herzl finally knew that he could not depend at all upon the support of the wealthy Jews. Writing to a colleague in

London, Herzl gave the order to organize the masses. That would be his way of showing the Rothschilds that the Zionist idea would work, even without them.

Back home in Vienna, Herzl plunged himself totally into his Zionist work. Supporters from all over the world dropped by to visit. Because the press of visitors was so great, Herzl joked that the path to the Promised Land went through his house in Vienna. Throughout Europe, Jews were forming Zionist groups to further the cause. In spite of all this strenuous activity, Herzl did not feel well. Physically and emotionally he showed signs of depression: He had difficulty breathing and always felt tired.

For all the changes in his life, one thing remained the same: his employment at the *Neue Freie Presse*. His salary was much less than when he was the Paris correspondent, but his value to the paper was still very great, although Herzl never really realized it. In spite of all the publicity he would attract as the Zionist leader, Herzl lived in constant fear of losing his job with the paper. Herzl was certainly not a poor man, yet he was the main financial contributor to his Zionist cause. The wages he received from the newspaper went to support his family. His connection with the paper had another significance as well. Being on the staff of one of Europe's most influential newspapers could open many doors for him on behalf of the Zionist cause. His editors were never impressed with his Jewish activities. Once, Herzl proudly showed one of the editors a press clipping about Zionism that had appeared in an American newspaper. The editor looked at him disparagingly and said, "You are driving the whole world crazy. A real Pied Piper of Hamelin."[22]

Herzl eventually established his own Zionist newspaper, *Die Welt* (*The World*). To announce the first issue on June 4, 1897, he even had to pay for an advertisement in the *Presse*. In effect, he was now working full time for two newspapers. Aside from being the new newspaper's main financial supporter, Herzl also edited, reported, and wrote

71

The first meeting of the Zionist newspaper
Die Welt *(The World). Herzl, at center,*
was the founder and editor.

editorials for it. In order not to offend his editors on the *Presse,* many of the articles he wrote for *Die Welt* were published anonymously or under assumed names. *Die Welt* never made any money or even began to rival the *Presse,* but it did become an important tool for spreading Zionist news to Jews all over Europe. Herzl was working harder than ever and driving himself to near exhaustion.

Herzl may have had problems with wealthy Jews, but the disagreements with his fellow Zionists proved to be even more irksome. Some of his early supporters felt he was becoming too aggressive. Colonel Goldsmid and the

British Lovers of Zion were getting nervous about Herzl's political action. They were afraid this activity would threaten the position the Jews had gained as equal citizens in their own countries. Even Rabbi Güdemann, one of Herzl's original supporters, was now much less enthusiastic. The rabbi, probably under the influence of the rich Jews of Vienna, even wrote a strongly anti-Zionist pamphlet.

But other early followers maintained their loyalty. Zionists in Europe and America continued to work feverishly. Hechler and Nevlinski were constantly in the background laying the groundwork for Herzl's further diplomatic work.

7

"AT BASEL I FOUNDED THE JEWISH STATE"

At Basel I founded the Jewish State.
If I said this out loud today, I would be
answered by universal laughter. Perhaps
in five years, and certainly in fifty,
everyone will know it.

Theodor Herzl

Herzl knew that the next step would be to organize the Zionist movement and to create a central structure. To that end he proposed to convene a congress of Zionists from all over the world. This would not be any ordinary gathering or discussion group but, as Herzl described it, a Jewish national assembly. For the first time in nearly two thousand years, there would be a formal meeting of Jews where, finally, the Jews would begin to take control of their destiny as a people. Herzl did not underestimate the effect this Congress would have not only upon Jews but upon the world. It would be a symbol of a new Jewish spirit that sought to overcome the persecution and discrimination of the past by creating a political force capable of leading the Jews to action.

74

To set up the Congress, Herzl drew upon his experiences as a reporter who had observed parliamentary organization in Paris. He knew that the Congress had to project an image of seriousness to the watching world. At the same time, the delegates had to feel that their work was of historic importance. Knowing how crucial every aspect of this Congress would be, Herzl, despite his deteriorating health, personally attended to the thousands of details necessary to arrange a meeting of such magnitude. Meanwhile, throughout Europe, previously independent Zionist groups were banding together under Herzl's leadership, and his words provided an almost hypnotic lure—"If we will it, it is no dream!"

In his diary, Herzl listed the problems he faced in organizing the Congress. He compared himself to someone trying to dance through a minefield of eggs:

1. *The egg of the* Neue Freie Presse, *which I must not compromise or furnish with a pretext for easing me out*
2. *Egg of the Orthodox*
3. *Egg of the Modernists*
4. *Egg of Austrian patriotism*
5. *Egg of Turkey, of the Sultan*
6. *Egg of the Russian government against which nothing unpleasant must be said, although the deplorable situation of the Russian Jews will have to be mentioned*
7. *Egg of the Christian denominations on account of the Holy Places.*

And to these he added several more:

Egg (of) Edmond de Rothschild; egg (of) Lovers of Zion in Russia; egg of the settlers, whose help from de Rothschild must not be spoiled for them; egg of

envy and jealousy. I must conduct the movement im-
personally and yet cannot let the reins out of my hands.
It is, one of the labors of Hercules . . . for which I no
longer have any zest.[23]

Herzl and his advisers met often in Vienna to organize
plans for the Congress. They originally selected August 25,
1897 as the date. The carefully chosen place was Munich,
Germany. Munich's location made it accessible to delegates from all over Europe. There were also many hotel
rooms and Kosher restaurants. But the Jews of Munich
would have nothing to do with such a Congress in their
city. They feared that holding the Congress there would
compromise their own image as loyal German citizens. So,
reluctantly, the site of the Congress was changed to Basel,
Switzerland with the meeting scheduled for August 29–31.

Invitations were printed in a number of languages and
were sent to Zionists throughout the world. Zionist workers
in many countries visited even the most isolated villages
where Jews lived to spread the word. Almost immediately,
delegates from Europe, Asia, Africa, and America began
responding. In Russia, where Zionist activity had been the
greatest, delegates planned their trips to Basel, even though
they knew that their government might interfere with
travel plans.

As the delegates gathered in Basel, all the details so
carefully arranged by Herzl were evident. Herzl arrived four
days before the Congress was to begin. When he first saw
the hall that had been rented for the Congress, he was
aghast. It was a garish vaudeville theater! This would never
do. Quickly, Herzl arranged the rental of the Municipal
Casino, an impressive hall that projected the image of
serious formality that he wanted for the Congress. As Herzl
stood outside the building, the thought occurred to him
that something was missing—a flag. Every nation needed
its own flag, and this was to be the first international con-
vocation of Jews in two thousand years. In a moment of

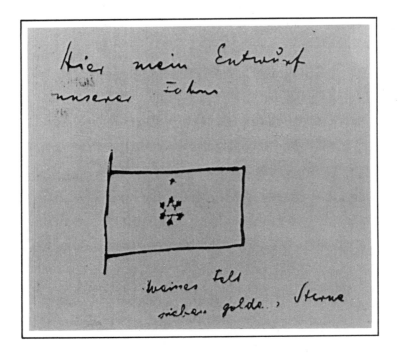

An early sketch of what was to become
the banner of the Zionist movement,
and later, the Israeli flag.

inspiration, David Wolffsohn, one of Herzl's earliest confidants, created the banner that not only served as the flag of the Zionist movement but ultimately became the flag of the new Jewish state. His idea was a simple one. From the traditional prayer shawl he took two blue bars placed on a white background. In the center, he placed a blue star of David. As delegates entered the hall and gazed at the flag, it seemed to them as if it had always existed as the symbol of the Jewish people. No one imagined that it was designed only hours earlier.

From the beginning, Herzl viewed the Congress as the parliament of the Jewish nation. He himself acted as the head of State. He made official diplomatic calls on Swiss

government officials, and, in turn, the citizens of Basel demonstrated the highest respect for the Zionist Congress and its delegates.

The Congress opened officially at nine o'clock on the morning of August 29, 1897. The delegates assembled in a spirit of self-conscious excitement. This was a momentous event in the long history of the Jewish people. Herzl had prepared the scene well. All the delegates were formally dressed. The men wore dress suits with tails and white ties, and the women in attendance wore evening gowns. Although it was morning, Herzl wished the Congress to present an image of dignity and importance to the entire world.

Finally, the moment everyone was waiting for had arrived. Dr. Theodor Herzl was introduced. Without emotion he walked slowly and quietly toward the podium. Thunderous applause rocked the hall accompanied by a stamping of feet and exuberant waving of handkerchiefs. The applause grew in intensity as Herzl moved forward; as in his earlier appearances, some in the audience tried to kiss his hand. Shouts of "Long live the king! Long live Herzl!" were heard throughout the hall. The cheering and applause continued for fifteen minutes as Herzl stood calmly on the stage facing the delegates. He did not bow, wave, or otherwise acknowledge their tribute. That would not have been dignified. With his body erect and his head held high, he continued to gaze solemnly at the delegates. To all who witnessed the scene, Herzl looked every bit like a leader.

Finally, the noise abated and Herzl began to speak. Slowly and distinctly he told the delegates, "We are here

*Herzl, in formal attire,
on his way to address the
first Zionist Congress.*

79

Herzl, surrounded by delegates in the Municipal Casino in Basel, presiding over the first session

to lay the foundation stone of the house which is to shelter the Jewish nation."

For three days the delegates met in formal and informal sessions. Among the two hundred delegates were three Christians, including the Reverend Hechler. Count de Nevlinski was also there, but not as a delegate. Newspaper reporters from all over the world attended and recorded the happenings. Within days readers in New York, London, and Germany were learning about the First Zionist Congress which Herzl had, almost single-handedly, engineered.

Once, while Dr. Nordau was presiding, Herzl made his way to the back of the hall. Suddenly he was overcome with emotion as he saw the green draped table on the platform, the raised seats of the officers, the journalist's table, and the dignified looking delegates. It really looked and felt like the parliament of the Jewish nation in session.

The work of the First Zionist Congress gave direction to the future of the Zionist movement. First, the delegates established the World Zionist Organization, with the Congress as its main deliberative body. Dr. Theodor Herzl was elected the first President. An "Actions Committee," to meet in Vienna under Herzl's direction, was also established to run the organization between Congresses. The organization was loosely structured to accommodate members from countries like Russia where international organizations were outlawed.

Secondly, a formal method of representation was established. Anyone who made a yearly membership payment called a *shekel*, after the Biblical coin, could vote for Congress delegates. The *shekel* was determined to be the equivalent of a half-dollar—modest enough to encourage all people to participate.

Thirdly, a plan was adopted by which Herzl's political aims could be implemented. This plan represented a compromise by all the different Zionist factions present and became the foundation for the entire movement. It was called simply, "The Basel Program." In clear terms it stated the goal of the Zionist movement as the establishment of a home for the Jewish people in Palestine secured by international law and recognition.

By the end of the Congress, most delegates had barely slept. When there were no formal sessions, informal meetings and discussions were held throughout Basel. As Herzl finally proclaimed the closing of the First Zionist Congress, the applause and cheers were deafening. Although the delegates were exhausted, they suddenly came alive with impromptu dancing, singing, and foot stomping. People embraced and hugged one another. Cries of "Next year in Jerusalem!" were heard amid the noise. Throughout the hall people joined in the singing of a Zionist song, "Hatikvah" (Hope),[24] which later became the Israeli national anthem.

No one, delegate or observer, could doubt the success of this first Congress. For Herzl, it was a dream come true. He had created the Society of Jews as he originally envisioned it in *The Jewish State*. For the dozens of isolated and independent Zionist groups, like the Lovers of Zion, there now existed a united worldwide organization with a leadership, constitution, and formal plan of action. For the Jewish people as a whole, there was now the first Jewish political assembly in two thousand years. It gave Jews a new feeling of self-confidence. And for the world in general there was a new positive image of the Jew. Israel Zangwill described the impact of the Congress this way:

> By the rivers of Babylon we sat down and wept as we remembered Zion.
> By the river of Basel we sat down resolved to weep no more!

A frequently reproduced photo of Herzl gazing out at the Rhine river in Basel

A few days later, back in Vienna, Herzl, aware of the historical image of the Congress, wrote in his diary:

Were I to sum up the Basel Congress in a word—which I shall guard against pronouncing publicly—it would be this: At Basel I founded the Jewish State. If I said this out loud today, I would be answered by universal laughter. Perhaps in five years, and certainly in fifty, everyone will know it.[25]

The First Zionist Congress was a truly momentous event. Now Herzl needed to build on this foundation and enlarge his base of support. Within a year the number of Zionist groups around the world had increased dramatically. The various committees appointed at the Congress were working on their specific tasks, and the circulation of the Zionist newspaper, *Die Welt*, largely financed by Herzl himself, had also grown modestly.

Just a year later, when the Second Zionist Congress was called to order, the number of delegates, now formally elected, had almost doubled and also included a large number of women delegates with equal voting power, an unusual event for the time.

One incident clearly illustrates the new self-image of the Zionists. At the opening of the Second Congress, just as the blue-and-white Zionist flag was being raised, a small parade of uniformed Swiss, celebrating a national holiday, marched past the congress hall. Instinctively and with great dignity, they shouted, "Long live the Jews!" To Herzl and the other Zionists who witnessed the scene, this was an unusually stirring and welcome sight.

Now that the movement was under way there was a need for real funding. Money was needed to run the day-to-day operations of the Zionist Organization, which up to now had been supported out of Herzl's own pocket. Once Jews were ready to settle in Palestine, even more money would be needed. Herzl did not like the idea of charitable grants, which Rothschild had established to support Jewish settlements in Palestine. Herzl's intention now was to establish a Jewish Colonial Bank to free Jews from any dependence upon the rich. Herzl, working with his colleague David Wolffsohn, contacted important Jewish bankers to enlist their support. The results were disappointing. Just as with his earlier experiences with the rich, he knew he would have to turn again to the masses for support, through the Congress.

But Herzl's energies were directed mainly toward diplomatic efforts. For the remainder of his life, in between Congresses, he spent much of his time traveling through Europe and the Middle East. He met with politicians and royalty, everywhere trying to gain recognition for the establishment of a Jewish homeland. He had not given up on Turkey. So, one of the first orders of business when the Second Zionist Congress opened in Basel in August, 1898 was a resolution in praise of the Turkish Sultan. A few days later, as the Congress ended, Herzl received a gracious acknowledgment from the Turkish ruler. The possibility of a diplomatic deal with Turkey was still alive.

An amusing sidelight of this Congress was that Herzl, at his expense of course, invited Nevlinski and his family to Basel to witness the Congress. Herzl hoped Nevlinski would then report to the Turks news of a financially secure and politically potent organization. Like many well-planned intentions, this one almost backfired when speaker after speaker rose to praise Herzl for doing such a great job with so little money!

—8—
OLD, TIRED, AND POOR

Nearly six years have passed since I
began this movement which has made me
old, tired, and poor.

Theodor Herzl

Herzl's diplomatic efforts now turned to Germany. In January, 1898, the Kaiser announced that he would make a visit to the Holy Land later that year. Through the intervention of Herzl's new friend, the Grand Duke of Baden, the Kaiser directed one of his aides, Count Philip zu Eulenburg, the German Ambassador to Vienna, to investigate the idea of a Jewish homeland in Palestine. Now, Herzl met with Eulenburg and the German Foreign Minister, Prince Bernhard von Bülow. The result was a promise that the Kaiser would receive Herzl in Jerusalem at the head of a Zionist delegation. In fact, the possibility also existed for the Kaiser to meet him, informally, during a stop-over in Constantinople. This was to Herzl's liking, for it would allow the Kaiser the opportunity to discuss Herzl's plans with his friend, the Sultan of Turkey.

Herzl was ecstatic but he was troubled by some practical problems. First, he had only a few days to form a delegation and make travel plans. Second, the Jewish Colonial Bank, which he hoped would provide the Zionist movement with financial clout, was not ready to begin operations. Finally, he was still worried about his job with the *Neue Freie Presse*. The movement had been eating away at his own and his family's savings, and he needed the job to keep his family solvent. Herzl was worried about having to take so many leaves of absence to travel on his Zionist business. This concern would continue to weigh on his mind terribly in the years to come as he constantly had to balance the needs of his Zionist work with his job.

Herzl understood the seriousness of this trip. To accompany him, he chose four important Zionists, each with a special expertise that would be needed to establish a new country. Dr. Max Bodenheimer, the President of the German Zionists, was a lawyer; Josef Seidener, the only person in the group who had been to Palestine before, was an engineer; Dr. Moritz Schnirer, Vice President of the "Actions Committee," was a physician; and David Wolffsohn, perhaps Herzl's closest adviser, was about to be named the head of the Jewish Colonial Bank.

The group arrived in Constantinople in mid-October, 1898. They were still not certain that the Kaiser would actually meet with Herzl there. They paced nervously in their hotel room until finally they received word that Dr. Herzl was to report to the Kaiser at four-thirty that afternoon. Ever aware of appearances, Herzl carefully chose his clothes and rented the most elegant coach the hotel could find to bring him to the palace that the Sultan had provided for the Kaiser. As Herzl, accompanied by Bodenheimer, arrived at the palace at the appointed time, they were stopped by menacing looking soldiers who allowed only Herzl to pass. Bodenheimer had to wait behind under armed guard.

The Kaiser, dressed in a striking black uniform, greeted Herzl amiably. Together, with only von Bülow present, both men freely discussed the possibilities of establishing a

Jewish homeland in Palestine under German protection. Even with all the positive words from the Kaiser about Zionism, Herzl, ever sensitive to the nuances of language, still detected undercurrents of anti-Semitism. The Kaiser, for example, thought that Jewish emigration might be a wonderful way to rid Germany of Jewish moneylenders! Herzl maintained a polite expression, but his blood boiled at the thought that even the Kaiser stereotyped all Jews as moneylenders. Von Bülow subtly kept the anti-Semitic undertones alive by injecting talk of anti-government activists, some of whom just happened to be Jewish. Nonetheless, both Herzl and the Kaiser were impressed with each other. Once, during the interview, Herzl turned to the Kaiser and confided, "I don't know—maybe I'm extremely stubborn about it—but the thing seems completely natural to me." The Kaiser instantly responded with enthusiasm, "To me, too!"[26]

As their conversation drew to a close, the Kaiser asked what Herzl would like him to request of the Sultan. Herzl said he wanted Turkish permission for a chartered company to establish a Jewish homeland in Palestine under German protection. "Good!" answered the Kaiser. "A chartered company!"[27]

After Bodenheimer was released from the palace guards, a pleased Herzl returned to the hotel. Although he was physically and emotionally drained and was complaining of heart palpitations, he sat down at the desk to compose the address he would deliver to the Kaiser when he met him officially in Jerusalem. This was von Bülow's idea. The audience in Jerusalem would be a public one, and the ever-cautious von Bülow wanted to make sure that Herzl would

Herzl, in October 1898,
heading for Palestine

88

Above: Herzl and some members of the Zionist delegation on board the freighter that took them to Palestine. Right: The delegates at the port of Jaffa.

say nothing that might embarrass the Kaiser or Germany's relationship with Turkey.

Herzl had to work quickly. The Germans expected a completed draft of the speech before the Kaiser left Constantinople. Besides, Herzl and his colleagues had to be on a ship for Palestine at eleven the next morning. It was the last possible ship that could get them there in time to meet the Kaiser.

On October 26, 1898, the small Zionist delegation arrived at the port of Jaffa. Herzl had remained on deck all night in anticipation of their arrival. As the Jaffa skyline came into view, Herzl awakened one of his traveling companions, David Wolffsohn. Overcome with emotion at this first glimpse of the ancient Jewish homeland, the men fell into each other's arms and, with tears in their eyes, whispered, "Our country! Our Mother Zion!" [28]

The initial excitement of reaching the Holy Land slowly gave way to disappointment as the five travelers, wearing white pith helmets, navigated themselves and their luggage through the teeming narrow streets. As they arrived exhausted and sweaty at their hotel, they heard the rumbling sound of cannon fire from the other side of the city. The Kaiser and his entourage had arrived.

Herzl visited several Jewish settlements begun by the Lovers of Zion: Mikveh Israel, an agricultural school, and Rishon le Zion, with its wine cellars financed by Rothschild. At Nes Ziona, the entire population turned out to greet him with bread, salt, and wine as children sang welcoming songs. But it was at Rehoboth that Herzl experienced an especially wonderful sight. As Herzl and his companions approached the village, a cavalcade of about twenty young men on horseback galloped toward them singing and cheering lustily in Hebrew. It was unbelievable! Vigorous young horsemen—not the European stereotype of young Jewish men. Herzl's eyes brimmed with tears as he thought of the promise this land held for the Jewish people and its young.

Herzl's old friend, the Reverend Hechler, was also on the scene. Taking advantage of the minister's connection at the German Court, Herzl sent Hechler to the Kaiser's marshal with the message that Herzl would be standing in front of the Mikveh Israel School the next morning where the Kaiser's procession was expected to pass.

At nine in the morning on October 29, Herzl, although not feeling well, stood on the road as planned. Near him were the other members of his party. Large crowds of men, women, and children lined the road waiting for a glimpse of the German ruler. Suddenly, in the distance, everyone could see a rising cloud of dust and the approach of uniformed men on horseback. The Kaiser was coming!

As the first group of heavily armed Turkish soldiers passed, Herzl gave a signal and the student chorus of the Mikveh Israel School began singing the German Imperial Anthem. The Kaiser, as soon as he saw Herzl, reined his horse toward him and bent down to shake hands. The two men exchanged pleasantries and spoke for a moment about the country's future and the need for water. After a few minutes, both shook hands again and the Kaiser began to ride off. In the background, the voices of the children's choir burst forth in a cheerful farewell song.

Wolffsohn was proud of the scene he had just witnessed. He was prouder still of the photographs he had taken of this breathtaking event. Unfortunately, when he had the film developed after his return to Jaffa, there was

The famous meeting between Herzl and Kaiser Wilhelm. The poor quality of the photo is the result of the photographer's nervousness. The shot is actually a reconstruction of two photos.

not one perfect picture. Later, the various sections were put together and a much reproduced version was fabricated.

Herzl and his colleagues made their way to Jerusalem aboard a cramped and steamy train. By the time the train crawled into the railroad station, Herzl was weak with a fever. Because it was a Friday evening and the onset of the Sabbath, Herzl, mindful of his religiously observant friends, would not ride further. Supported by his companions and leaning on a cane, he slowly inched his way toward their hotel and a refreshing night's sleep.

His first view of the Holy City by daylight left him with mixed feelings. Here before him was a city that had been allowed to deteriorate by its succession of conquerers. The air was heavy with dank and foul odors. Yet beneath it all, Herzl could easily envision Jerusalem restored as one of the world's most beautiful cities.

But Herzl was not in Jerusalem as a tourist. He had an appointment with one of the world's most important rulers. On November 2, Dr. Herzl and the official Zionist delegation were officially received by His Majesty, Wilhelm II, the Kaiser of Germany. Herzl had good reason to feel optimistic about the meeting. All the preliminary sessions with von Bülow, Eulenburg, and the Kaiser himself had seemed to indicate a willingness by Germany to support the creation of a Jewish homeland in Palestine. In a few minutes, Herzl's optimism would dramatically disappear.

Herzl introduced the members of the delegation and presented the Kaiser with an album of photographs showing the Jewish colonies in Palestine. Then, as planned, Herzl began reading the edited speech originally submitted in Turkey. Von Bülow, like the director of a school play, followed Herzl's reading, word for word, from his copy of the speech. The Kaiser politely thanked Herzl for his remarks and offered some general comments about the land and the need for water, just as he had done at their informal meeting on the road at Mikveh Israel. Herzl responded by saying that, although it would cost a lot of

*Herzl and members of the Zionist delegation in front
of the house they stayed in while in Jerusalem*

money, the Jews would be able to solve that problem. Both the Kaiser and von Bülow cheerfully responded with a few subtly snide remarks about Jews and money. Nothing further was mentioned about Germany's intervening with the Sultan to establish a Jewish state under German protection. Apparently, something had happened to cause the Kaiser to lose interest in Herzl's plan. Herzl and his companions were unprepared for this sudden indifference and, after taking leave of the Kaiser, left Palestine almost immediately.

Herzl was, to say the least, disappointed; but he did not despair. He sensed that Turkey was just not ready to accept a Jewish state in Palestine. Much more work lay ahead for the Zionists before Turkey and Germany would be persuaded to grant their support. Herzl continued his friendly relations with the Grand Duke of Baden, but he never again would discuss the Jewish homeland with the Kaiser.

Herzl continued to work harder for his cause. Although the numbers of Zionists and Zionist organizations were steadily growing, Herzl was, in effect, continuing to run a "one-man show" which Dr. Cyrus Adler, a noted American historian, referred to as "at once the source of its weakness and its strength. It would be an almost unique event in Jewish history, if a single man can carry through a great national plan without secession or conflict." [29]

Herzl was in constant motion. Like an experienced prizefighter, he moved alertly around the ring of European politics ever on the lookout for the advantage that would result in the ultimate prize of Palestine. While he still tried to arrange a meeting with the Sultan of Turkey, he took advantage of every opportunity to spread the word about Zionism. It seemed as if he were spending the greater part of his life traveling on the railroads of Europe. In June, 1899, he attended a Peace Conference in The Hague sponsored by Nicholas II, the Czar of Russia. The news from Russia was not good. Anti-Semitic violence seemed to continue unabated. To Herzl, this visit was yet another way to bring the Zionist message to world leaders.

His health was steadily deteriorating. When he addressed a meeting of Eastern European Jews in London's East End, he had just suffered a slight heart attack. But that did not prevent him from delivering an enthusiastic speech that roused the cheering audience to its feet when he asked if they believed that the Jews would go to Palestine if they got their land back.

This emotional enthusiasm endeared Herzl to the long suffering Jews of Eastern Europe. Ironically, a number of delegates to the Third Zionist Congress in Basel on August 1, 1899 did not share this positive feeling. They thought that Herzl was exciting the masses unduly, considering the fact that no real diplomatic success had been achieved to date.

Herzl began working even harder; he traveled, spoke, wrote letters, attended numerous meetings, and continued work on his Zionist newspaper, *Die Welt*. Money problems were constantly on his mind, both personally and with his organizations. His work on the *Neue Freie Presse* became even more tedious to him, but he dared not complain for fear of losing his job. And to earn more money, the busy Zionist leader returned to his old profession of writing plays.

The Fourth Zionist Congress was set for August, 1900. Unlike the previous three, which had been held in Switzerland, it was held in London. England occupied an important position in the world but exercised no influence at that time over Palestine. Little did Herzl realize that, less than twenty years later, it would be England and not Turkey that would hold the key to the Holy Land. In the meantime, Turkey remained Theodor Herzl's major diplomatic target.

In spite of the many successes he had accomplished to date, he felt emotionally unfulfilled, physically wasted, and financially drained. On May 2, 1901, he candidly revealed his feelings in his diary.

The Fourth Zionist Congress, August 1900. This was the first session held in London. Herzl is in the second row from the top, in the middle.

Today I am forty-one years old. . . . It is almost six years since I started this movement which has made me old, tired, and poor.[30]

To complicate matters, Count de Nevlinski, the man who had introduced Herzl to the intrigues of the Turkish Court, died. In his place, another political agent, Arminius Vámbéry, arrived on the scene. Now, only a few weeks after he had written that gloomy entry in his diary, Herzl received word through Vámbéry that Abdul Hamid, the Sultan of Turkey, was prepared to receive him in Constantinople.

On May 10, 1901, Herzl was once again on the Orient Express. Traveling with him were his old Zionist confidant, Wolffsohn, and another close aide, Oskar Marmorek. Turkey's financial condition had grown even worse since Herzl's first visit, and he hoped to exploit that problem in his negotiations with the Turks for a charter for Palestine. Although the Sultan was cordial, he did not commit himself on the issue of a Jewish homeland in Palestine. He did, however, state that small groups of Jews would be welcome to settle anywhere in the empire as long as they accepted Turkish citizenship. This was certainly not the charter Herzl wanted but, at least, it left the door still open for further negotiation. As a sign of his willingness to continue discussions, the Sultan presented Herzl with yet another royal decoration and, as a personal gift, a diamond stickpin. Although this meeting produced no tangible diplomatic breakthrough, the fact that it took place at all captured the attention of the Jewish world. Herzl's stature as a world Jewish leader was even further enhanced. At the same time, however, his financial concerns continued to grow.

If only he could raise a substantial amount of money, Herzl thought, the Sultan would be more enthusiastic about the idea of the charter. Money was also needed to provide "gifts" for large numbers of Turkish bureaucrats and officials. Unfortunately, bribery was a way of life in Turkey. As Herzl discovered, it was the only way to insure a proper reception by the ruling circles. Herzl referred to his "business" experiences in Turkey as dealing with Ali Baba and the Forty Thieves.

This was the only one of Herzl's several visits to Turkey during which he personally met with the Sultan. In his future visits, he negotiated with lower-level Turkish officials. Slowly, a revised immigration policy began to emerge. Unlimited numbers of Jews were still unwelcome in Palestine, but the Turkish government would not object to large Jewish settlements in other sections of the Turkish empire such as Mesopotamia. This was a step in the right direction, but Herzl would not accept anything less than a charter for Palestine.

In the end, all of Herzl's efforts in Turkey turned out to be in vain. For the Sultan and his advisers never had any intention of granting Herzl and the Jews any land in any territory ruled by the Ottoman Empire. They were merely leading Herzl on in order to make their international bankers nervous about a serious possibility of Jewish financing of the monstrous Turkish debt. Herzl was being used as a pawn in a game of high finance in order to reduce the interest rate on the loan Turkey was then negotiating with French bankers. Herzl still maintained contact with the officials he met in Turkey just as he did with the Germans he had met earlier. But for now, Herzl turned the focus of his diplomatic attention to England and, in particular, to the territory it controlled in Egypt.

The Fifth Zionist Congress was held in Basel between December 26 and 30, 1901. High on the agenda was a report by Herzl about his meeting with the Sultan. The delegates were particularly impressed with the reading of a friendly message to them from the Turkish ruler. The Zionist movement had grown tremendously since that first Congress in 1897 and was beginning to show signs of developing some serious inner conflicts. The largest and most vocal critical group was led by a noted Hebrew writer, Asher Ginsburg, better known by his pen name, Ahad Ha'Am (One of the People). He thought that Herzl and the political Zionists were not being realistic about the chances for an immediate establishment of a Jewish homeland. A Jewish state would certainly be a reality in the future, he argued. Until then, Zionism should focus on preparing Jews for a life in that new homeland based on Jewish ideas and values. He called his program "cultural Zionism," as opposed to Herzl's "political Zionism."

Debate at the Congress was vigorous and open, but Herzl, as president, controlled the outcome. While his "political Zionism" prevailed, compromises on both sides allowed the Zionist movement to remain united. Among the accomplishments of this Congress were the opening of the Jewish Colonial Bank and the founding of the Jewish National Fund. Both institutions received their major support from the masses, but their purposes differed. The bank funds were to be used to establish a Jewish homeland in Palestine; diplomatic expenses, emigration costs, and the establishing of industry and institutions in the new land were the bank's responsibility. The Jewish National Fund was established for the purchase of land in Palestine not in the name of individuals, but on behalf of the Jewish people as a whole. The little blue-and-white collection boxes of the Fund became fixtures in Jewish homes throughout the world. The kopeks, pennies, and farthings collected became the chief source of funds for the actual purchase of land in Palestine. Today, the JNF, as it is known, still plays an active role in Israeli life. It no longer purchases land but has major responsibility for the planting of trees and for irrigation and beautification of the State of Israel.

9

ON THE MARCH

*Zionism was the Jewish People
on the March*

Theodor Herzl

Herzl continued to feel pressured. His diplomatic efforts, while successful in opening channels of communication, had not yet yielded a Jewish homeland. Jews fleeing persecution in Eastern Europe continued to seek freedom in the countries of the West. But even in England, where acceptance of political refugees had become a tradition, questions about the new immigrants began to surface. Would these newcomers take jobs away from British citizens? How would they support themselves? In 1902, a Royal Commission was established to study the immigration problem in England. Zionists there saw this debate as a good opportunity to bring up the solution Zionism offered. If the Jews had their own country, this concern over their immigration would not exist. Herzl was invited to testify before the Commission and again traveled to London.

Before he had the opportunity to testify, Herzl received the sad news that his beloved father, Jacob, had died suddenly in Vienna. Emotionally drained, the mourning son quickly left London and returned to Vienna. Father and son had been particularly close. Jacob supported his son's Zionist activities, financially and spiritually. The younger Herzl knew he could always depend on his father for the right advice and counsel. Now, with his father gone, Theodor, ever confident that his dream of a Jewish state would come true, chose to have his father buried in a temporary grave in Vienna. Eventually, Jacob Herzl would be reburied in the new Jewish state along with his wife, son, and daughter.

Herzl returned to England certain that his visit would lead to a positive conclusion. His contacts with Turkey were still important to him, but he now began to explore a role for England in the establishment of a Jewish homeland. England controlled a great deal of territory in the Middle East near Palestine. Perhaps even a temporary refuge in Cyprus or in Egypt would help the British solve their Jewish immigration problem and induce the Turks to rethink their Palestine policy toward Jews.

Ironically, the only Jewish person on the Royal Commission was an English member of the wealthy Rothschild family to which Herzl had earlier unsuccessfully turned for support. Surprisingly, when a meeting between Herzl and Lord Rothschild took place, the results were more positive than either man could have imagined. While strongly asserting his opposition to Zionism, Rothschild listened to Herzl's arguments in favor of a Jewish colony in a British-controlled territory. It was not that Herzl had given up on Palestine, far from it. But his options were quite limited: Germany and Turkey held no promise for his dream of a Jewish homeland in Palestine. And the news from Russia about further anti-Semitic violence caused Herzl to look about for some temporary solution to save Jewish lives. When Rothschild, in an offhanded remark, suggested Uganda, a British territory in the heart of Africa, Herzl immediately refused. He would only accept land near Palestine. Lord Rothschild readily agreed and even volunteered to arrange a meeting for Herzl with the British Colonial Secretary, Joseph Chamberlain. When he met with Chamberlain several weeks later, Herzl had just returned from his last trip to Constantinople knowing that no hope now existed for a Turkish solution. It was England that held the key to at least a temporary home where Jews could find friendly refuge.

Chamberlain was most cordial and listened attentively to Herzl's proposal: a Jewish colony, administered by the Jews themselves, on British-owned land in Cyprus or El-Arish, near Palestine. Herzl then met with the British Foreign Minister, Lord Landsdowne, who reacted just as positively as Chamberlain. Cyprus was ruled out: Too many people of differing nationalities already lived there. El-Arish, though, was still a possibility. Its location was near Palestine, it was relatively uninhabited, and it was under British control. Before anything definite could be arranged, it was necessary to obtain the approval of the most important British official in the Middle East, Lord Cromer, the High Commissioner in Egypt.

Seeing the possibility of a real diplomatic success, Herzl rushed into action. He sent a trusted English Zionist, Leopold Greenberg, to meet with Lord Cromer in Egypt. At the same time, a commission was formed to investigate all the technical aspects of establishing a Jewish colony in El-Arish. On the Commission were Zionists as well as British and Egyptian experts. While Greenberg and the commission members conducted their business, an exhausted Herzl, weak and feverish, rested in a small Alpine village awaiting word of an agreement.

But agreement was not easy to obtain. The Commission's report was not totally favorable. Water, it seemed, was a major problem. There was not enough to support the needs of a large population. The problem was not unsolvable, however. Large amounts of water could be piped in, at great expense, from Egypt. But the Egyptians were not willing to give up their precious water, at any price. Herzl himself made an arduous journey to Egypt in an attempt to salvage the situation. He wrote a detailed proposal to Lord Cromer and, in response, the door was kept open for further discussion. In fact, the negotiations between the British government and the Zionist movement took on the appearance and form of serious state-to-state diplomacy. Herzl felt optimistic. While it was true that El-Arish was not the Holy Land, a great world power was dealing with the Zionists on a diplomatic level not reached by Jews in modern times. A colony in El-Arish would provide the safe haven East European Jews most needed at that time. Herzl thought it might somehow also persuade the Turkish Sultan to reconsider the Zionist plans for Palestine.

Despite Herzl's strong persuasive powers, Lord Cromer's final report to London was negative. There would be no Jewish colony, even on a temporary basis, at El-Arish. It was not just Egyptian concern about water that doomed the idea; there were other very serious political considerations. Herzl received the bad news in a meeting with the Colonial Secretary in London on April 23, 1903. Chamberlain, trying to boost Herzl's spirits, offered a suggestion. "I have seen a land for you on my travels—Uganda. It's hot on the coast but farther inland the climate becomes excellent, even for Europeans. . . . And I thought to myself, that would be a land for Dr. Herzl. But of course he wants only to go to Palestine or its vicinity."

"Yes, I have to," Herzl responded.[31] But this was the second time the East African country of Uganda had come up in conversation—the first time with Lord Rothschild. Herzl did not then realize how central Uganda would soon become in his life.

Totally disillusioned and with no other opportunities in sight, Theodor Herzl sadly returned to Vienna. In total despair, he now bought a family burial vault. He had absolutely no hope of ever reburying his father in Palestine.

Herzl, in increasingly failing health, attended the reburial. As his father's casket was lowered into its permanent resting place, a forlorn Herzl turned to a friend and, making a gesture at the open grave, prophetically stated, "Soon, very soon, I too shall lie down there."

Herzl constantly drew upon his own rich literary talents to spread the lessons of Zionism. He had written newspaper articles, plays, *The Jewish State*, and numerous speeches. In 1899, he began work on a novel which he called, in German, *Altneuland*, or *Old-New Land*. The title came from the name of the famous synagogue in Prague, the *Altneuschul* (Old-New Synagogue). In the novel, Herzl described life in the new Jewish homeland as he envisioned it several decades hence. It was a utopia—a perfect society with ideal political, economic, and social conditions. People of all backgrounds lived harmoniously with one another; everyone was productively employed. Anti-Semitism was unknown there and had greatly diminished in other countries by virtue of this new country's moral and cultural perfection. In science and technology, the country was in the forefront of inventiveness, making the utmost use of science for the benefit of mankind.

The motto Herzl chose for this book soon became the slogan of the entire Zionist movement. Its words symbolized the hope and fervor of the cause. "If you will it, it is no dream."

Herzl wanted *Altneuland* to impress the world with the fact that the Jews were like everyone else. Given the right opportunities and their own country, they could become living examples of progressive human achievement.

Rather than unite the Zionists, however, his book tended only to widen the gap that existed among the Zionist factions. The group led by Ahad Ha'Am became even more vocal in opposition to Herzl's political approach. In *Altneuland* they saw proof that Herzl did not understand the rich culture and tradition that had united Jews for centuries. This new land, after all, was described by

Herzl only in secular, technological and scientific terms. There was nothing Jewish about it!

Among those agreeing with Ahad Ha'Am was Chaim Weizmann, who later would become the first president of the State of Israel. Weizmann wrote that many of the Lovers of Zion—followers of Ahad Ha'Am—considered Herzl naive at the time. Perhaps he was, but fifty years later Herzl's *Altneuland* ultimately came to life as the new State of Israel.

To a modern world numbed by the horrors of the Holocaust, what happened in the little Russian town of Kishinev in 1903 seems almost unimportant. Yet, to the world of that time, the name of Kishinev and the story of what happened there had the same impact as Auschwitz. In a particularly brutal pogrom, nearly fifty Jews were murdered and thousands more savagely attacked. Women were raped and children were beaten. Jewish property was destroyed. The attacks took place during the Easter weekend, a traditional time for anti-Semitic attacks in Russia. But the pogrom was not totally religious in nature. It was well planned and directed by Russian government officials partially as a warning to Jews. There was a growing revolutionary movement in Russia; many of the activists were Jewish. A little violence, the Russians thought, might weaken this anti-government activity. But the attacks soon became front page news throughout Europe and the United States. The entire civilized world was shocked. Condemnation of the event and Russian treatment of Jews was almost universal. The Russians were genuinely surprised at this hostile reaction.

Herzl was more than dismayed. Here were hundreds of thousands of Jews in constant danger, and there was no place for them to go. Palestine was out of reach; El-Arish was impossible. It was at this point that the previously unthinkable Uganda territory began to look more inviting. At least it would provide a temporary escape hatch for the suffering Jews of Eastern Europe. Herzl ordered his El-Arish negotiator, Greenberg, to open discussions with the British on the East African territory.

Meanwhile, Herzl requested and finally obtained permission to visit Russia. On August 7, 1903, he arrived in Russia. He hoped to advance the Zionist cause in the very country where anti-Semitism seemed to be government policy. He met with the Minister of the Interior, Vyacheslav Plehve, the person considered by many responsible for the Kishinev massacre, and with Count Witte, the Minister of Finance. Both men were most friendly and were receptive to Herzl's ideas. Strange as it was, the anti-Semites of the world seemed to be the most ardent supporters of Zionism. They liked the idea of the Jewish state. It was only the Jews that they hated! For different reasons, they shared with Herzl the same goal of wanting to remove Jews from Eastern Europe. Their methods also differed. In an attempt to be statesmanlike, Count Witte told Herzl about a comment he had made to the Czar. He would, he recounted, be perfectly happy to drown six or seven million Jews in the Black Sea, but since that wasn't possible, the Russians just had to let the Jews live—preferably away from Russia!

The Russian Zionists had also come upon hard times. The government was clamping down on their organizational activities and fund raising: Police, under Plehve's control, were breaking up their meetings. Herzl secured assurance from Plehve that the police would no longer interfere with the activity of the Russian Zionists. If nothing else, this assurance alone was worth the trip. But the greatest impact of all was on Herzl himself. For the first time since he had begun his Zionist work, Herzl got to see the Russian Jews and their situation through direct observation. He visited the homes of the poor and saw at firsthand the poverty and despair that made the Russian Jews the most fervent and active Zionists in the world. He now understood what he had begun to see at the Zionist Congresses: the inner strength that allowed these Jews to survive their terrible situation.

The Jews of Russia welcomed Herzl as a conquering hero. Wherever he went crowds of enthusiastic Jews thronged about him or lined his route. In an emotion-filled welcome to the city of Vilna by the leaders of the Jewish community, Herzl was nearly moved to tears. Even at one o'clock in the morning, as he rode through the dark streets of the city, thousands of Jews lined the way to the railroad station to bid Herzl farewell. While the police tried to keep the crowds back, people surged forward for a last look at the living Jewish legend who had given them such hope. As the train pulled out, Herzl shouted out to the Jewish leaders of Vilna not to lose courage, that better times were coming.

What Herzl did not say was that in his pocket was a letter of great importance. It had just reached him during his visit in Vilna. The letter was from Sir Clement Hill of the British Foreign Office and represented the diligent work of Greenberg in London. The letter formally invited the Zionists to send an official delegation to Uganda to choose suitable land on which to establish a Jewish colony under British protection. The colony would have a Jewish governor and be self-governing on domestic issues. The significance of this letter went beyond the offer of land. It was the first official recognition of the Zionist movement as the legal representative of the Jewish people. The land in question was not the Holy Land, but to Herzl it offered just what he thought was needed at the moment—a temporary home for Jewish people in need. He could not have foreseen the intense storm of dissent this letter would soon unleash in the Zionist world.

At the Fifth Zionist Congress in December, 1901, it had been decided that all future Congresses would be held only every two years. So now, two years later, in August,

The Sixth Zionist Congress, 1903, in Basel. Herzl is in the center with his mother to his left.

1903, the Sixth Zionist Congress convened in Basel. It was to be Herzl's last Congress. It was the largest yet and was destined to be the most controversial. Herzl was tired and his heart palpitations grew worse. He was not prepared for the anger that was intensifying around him.

Herzl was certain that the delegates would greet the news of the "historic" letter from the British Government with profound relief. Finally something tangible could be done to aid their distressed Russian brethren. But as soon as he presented the letter to the Actions Committee a day before the opening session, he realized that his optimism had been short-lived. While most of the delegates from the Western countries supported Herzl and his Uganda plan, the Russians, those most affected by this plan, were violently opposed. First, they could not understand how Herzl could have met with their worst enemy, the man who ordered the Kishinev massacre. Secondly, to them there was but one Jewish homeland and its name was Palestine. Nothing less—or else—would do, no matter what humanitarian reasons were offered.

The next day Herzl officially opened the Congress, and his remarks received polite applause. He reviewed the work of the past two years and spoke about the desperate needs of the Russian Jews. He then turned to the pressing issue of Uganda. In a calm voice, he told the delegates that he understood very well that this British-ruled African territory was certainly not Zion. But in view of the difficulties, it was a generous offer from the British government that should not be refused. With this temporary haven, which Nordau called a "night shelter," the Zionists would be in a stronger position to obtain Palestine eventually. Herzl made a motion to appoint a committee to evaluate the Uganda proposal. The motion passed by a vote of 295 to 178 with 99 delegates abstaining. But the empty victory quickly turned sour as the opposing delegates marched out of the Congress. Pandemonium broke out in the hall. Many delegates were openly sobbing and embracing one another in uncontrollable grief. Leading the "mourners" were the Jews of Russia, from Kishinev and Vilna; they were the ones who would have benefited most from the Uganda plan. For them, however, there could be no Jewish state without Palestine. They understood, perhaps even more than Herzl, that the centuries-old Jewish yearning for a return to Zion could not be diverted from the Holy Land to Africa.

The Russians and their supporters moved to a nearby room. There they continued their mourning. Many of them sat on the floor in the traditional position of one who has just lost a close family member. Herzl knew he had to do something to prevent the World Zionist Organization from breaking up. A divided movement would not give him the negotiating power he needed in the arena of world politics. He decided to meet personally with the protestors.

Making his way to their meeting room, Herzl knocked on the door and called out his name. At first the incensed demonstrators would not admit him. They actually took a vote on whether or not to let him in before finally allowing him to enter. As he strode into the room, one man yelled, "Traitor!" The shaken leader walked purposely to the front of the room and pleaded with them calmly, yet persuasively, not to destroy everything for which they had worked. He explained again that he understood their feelings and promised to continue working with them for the eventual establishment of a Jewish state in Palestine.

The next morning the dissenters returned to the Congress Hall. Herzl was reelected president by an overwhelming majority with only three votes cast against him. In his closing speech, he repeated that the Uganda plan was only a temporary measure. And in a dramatic gesture to symbolize his promise of the night before, he raised his right hand and recited, in Hebrew, these words from the Psalms: "If I forget thee, O Jerusalem, may my right hand forget its cunning!"[32] To the applause of the delegates, Herzl banged the gavel down and closed the last Congress he would ever attend.

Later that day, in a reflective mood, Herzl sat in a hotel room with his closest advisors. As they sipped mineral water, Herzl, in a state of almost total collapse, spoke about the future. He was ready, at the next Congress, to step down from the presidency but still be ready to help out, if, as he said, "I live till then." At that time he planned to end his public speech with these words: "By what I have done, I have not made Zionism poorer, but Jewry richer. Farewell!" He would not live long enough to deliver that parting sentiment.

The Uganda proposal resolved itself within a short time much as the El-Arish plan had. British settlers and government officials were opposed to a mass immigration of Jews, and soon London began backing away from its original position. The Jews were thus free once more to consider only Palestine as the Jewish homeland. But the Uganda letter from the British government was a milestone in Jewish history. Just thirteen years later, with the British now in actual control of Palestine, another letter from the British government, known simply as the Balfour Declaration, became the "Charter" Herzl had so intensely sought. In it, Lord Balfour, the British Foreign Minister, provided the Zionists with the international recognition that led directly to the establishment of the modern State of Israel in 1948. With a few simple words, the die was cast for Herzl's Jewish state: "His Majesty's Government view with favour the establishment in Palestine of a national home for the Jewish people. . . ."[33]

Throughout many years, Herzl had been working continuously to the point of ultimate collapse. The Uganda affair had certainly not helped his failing heart. He remained constantly on guard against the challenges to his leadership from the Russian Zionists. At the same time, he kept the entire organization going, traveled constantly across Europe meeting with world leaders, and, to his great distaste, kept churning out articles for his employers at the *Neue Freie Presse*. He maintained relations with his old diplomatic contacts and continued to make new ones. In December, he made a new offer to the Turkish Sultan for a charter to colonize a section of Palestine near Acre. At the same time, he turned to the Vatican and Italy for support.

In early 1904, a haggard Herzl, oblivious to his deteriorating condition, traveled to Italy. He had a warm and sympathetic meeting with the King of Italy, Victor Emannuel III. The King offered his assistance freely to Herzl and the Zionist cause. Herzl's meeting with the Pope was less encouraging.

Pope Pius X, leader of the world's Roman Catholics,

received Dr. Theodor Herzl in a lengthy private audience on January 25. The Pope clearly stated that he could not support the return of the Jews to the Holy Land as long as they did not embrace Christianity. "The Jewish people have not recognized our Lord," he lectured the Zionist leader: "therefore we cannot recognize the Jewish people."[34]

The establishment of a Jewish homeland in Palestine had been Herzl's dream from the beginning. His willingness to negotiate for a temporary home in El-Arish, Mesopotamia, and Uganda only proved his deep concern for the safety of the Jewish people. He knew that without a land of their own, the Jews would always be considered strangers wherever they lived. To him, also, the colonization of Palestine by small groups supported by charity was not in the best interest of the Jewish people. Only diplomatic recognition by the world powers of a Jewish homeland could lead to the "normalization" of the Jewish condition. This was the goal to which Herzl had devoted the last nine years of his life. His obsession with achieving this goal contributed in large measure to his untimely death.

By May, 1904, he had suffered several slight heart attacks and was under the constant care of several doctors. On May 9, as he was walking with one of his doctors, he suffered another attack. Herzl, who well understood the seriousness of his physical condition, turned to the doctor and plaintively said he hoped that he hadn't been too bad a servant of his movement.

At Edlach, Austria, high in the mountains where the doctors had sent him to rest, Theodor Herzl died on July 3, 1904. He was only forty-four years old.

Just prior to his death, Herzl was visited by his mother, wife, and children. Zionist leaders from all over Europe arrived to be close to their dying leader. Hechler, his first and most loyal follower, also came to comfort him. To the impassioned minister, Herzl made a final request. "Greet everyone for me—I gave my life for my people."[35]

Herzl's funeral procession
on July 7, 1904

His funeral on July 7 was one of the largest Vienna had ever seen. From throughout Europe Jews of all backgrounds and classes gathered to pay their last respects. According to the instructions he had left in his will, Herzl was buried in a metal coffin next to his beloved father, "to remain there until the Jewish people will transfer my remains to Palestine." His long time colleague and successor, David Wolffsohn, in a choked voice, publicly repeated the words of the Psalm Herzl had recited at the close of the Sixth Zionist Congress. "If I forget thee, O Jerusalem, may my right hand lose its cunning."[36]

Herzl was gone. But his dream lived on and came true.

EPILOGUE
A ROMANTIC TALE

*The last seven years had the
character of a romantic tale.*

Ahad Ha'Am

The unexpected death of Theodor Herzl came as a profound shock to Jews around the world. His loss was deeply felt. He not only made the Jews aware of themselves, he also taught them to rely on their own initiative. For centuries Jews had tried to survive oppression by keeping to themselves. Then Theodor Herzl came to the public and called them into action. He reminded Jews that they were equal to all other people and like other people deserved a land of their own. Taking a leaderless group of idealists, he molded them into an internationally recognized political force.

To Herzl, Zionism was "a return to Judaism." By focusing on the reestablishment of the Jewish state, he instilled a sense of pride in his fellow Jews—a feeling they had not experienced much over the previous two thousand years.

Many considered Herzl the uncrowned leader of world Jewry. Few remembered that he had begun his labors for his people only nine years earlier. Even Ahad Ha'Am, the writer who had vigorously opposed many of the Zionist leader's ideas, recognized Herzl's special impact on the world. "The last seven years," he wrote, "had the character of a romantic tale."

Although Herzl's dream of a homeland did not materialize during his lifetime, he left behind the blueprint that, fifty years later, resulted in the State of Israel.

While Herzl was alive, he traveled throughout Europe in an attempt to obtain diplomatic recognition for his cause. Within a decade after his death, the world had been turned upside down. Each of the countries Herzl had negotiated with would soon be totally involved in the horrible conflict of World War I. Germany would be totally defeated; her ally, Turkey, would lose its empire, including Palestine. Russia would find itself heavily embroiled in the revolution that had been simmering for years. The Czar, Plehve, the Kaiser, and the Sultan were unceremoniously erased from the world scene.

Only England remained dominant. At the conclusion of World War I, Palestine fell under the control of the British, acting under a mandate from the League of Nations. The groundwork laid by Herzl and the Zionists in England paid off as England formally recognized, in the Balfour Declaration, the right of the Jewish people to a national homeland in Palestine. It would take several more decades of strife, negotiations, and political maneuvering until an independent Jewish state could be proclaimed. And when that proclamation was made to the world on May 14, 1948 by David Ben Gurion, it was under a huge portrait of the man responsible for Israel's rebirth as a nation—Theodor Herzl.

Herzl's private life was marked by unhappiness and frustration. His marriage was a constant source of heartache to him. His children, whom he adored but had little time for, each met a tragic end. Pauline, the eldest, was a drug addict and suffered from mental disease. She died in 1930.

Theodor Herzl's gravesite in Jerusalem, on a
hillside that now bears his name, Mount Herzl

Hans, the only son, committed suicide shortly thereafter. Trude, the youngest, also had psychiatric problems. She married, however, and had a son. She died in a Nazi concentration camp in 1943. Her son, who became a British army officer, committed suicide in 1946 by jumping off a bridge in Washington, D.C. where he had been attached to the British Embassy. His death marked the end of the Herzl family line.

In spite of his family's personal tragedy, Theodor Herzl left behind another kind of legacy—a vibrant, creative and self-assured Jewish people reestablished in their own land. This land and its people serve as a constant reminder of Herzl's vision and hope. Standing on Mt. Herzl, surrounded by the panorama of modern Israel, a visitor today can glance down at the simple gravesite of Theodor Herzl and instantly understand the significance of his powerful yet eloquent words: "If you will it, it is no dream!"

NOTES

1. JTA Daily News Bulletin, Vol. XVI, No. 189, August 18, 1949.

2. JTA Daily News Bulletin, Vol. XVI, No. 188, August 17, 1949.

3. Amos Elon, *Herzl* (New York: Holt, Rinehart and Winston, 1975), p. 16.

4. Theodor Herzl, "Experiences and Moods: An Autobiographic Sketch," *Theodor Herzl: A Memorial*, edited by Meyer W. Weisgal (New York: The New Palestine, 1929), p. 183.

This book, *Theodor Herzl: A Memorial*, is a researcher's treasure trove containing firsthand recollections of Herzl by the people who actually knew him—his colleagues. The book was reprinted in 1976 by Hyperion Press, Inc., 47 Riverside Avenue, Westport, CT 06880.

5. A feuilleton (fe-ye-to) was a popular feature article that appeared in European newspapers and magazines. It was written to entertain the reader with a reporter's wit and philosophy on a variety of subjects.

6. Betty Schechter, *The Dreyfus Affair, A National Scandal* (Boston: Houghton Mifflin Company, 1965), p. 55.

7. Hermann Bahr, "The Fateful Moment," *Theodor Herzl: A Memorial*, edited by Meyer W. Weisgal, p. 67.

Hermann Bahr, who was one of Herzl's closest friends, was the fraternity member in Vienna who delivered the fiery anti-Semitic speech that drove Herzl from his membership in Albia.

8. Hermann Bahr, "The Fateful Moment," *Theodor Herzl: A Memorial*, p. 68.

9. *The Diaries of Theodor Herzl*, edited by Marvin Lowenthal (New York: The Dial Press, 1956), p. 16.

During his lifetime, Theodor Herzl authored numerous plays, dramas and newspaper features. Today, nearly all those works are forgotten. It is ironic that of all his literary accomplishments, the diaries he began keeping in 1895 survive as his major written legacy. These detailed volumes provide a unique firsthand look at the development of early Zionism as well as an intimate view of the founder himself.

Over the years the diaries have been excerpted and translated into a number of languages from the original German. Several editions of his excerpted diaries have appeared in English, including one edited by Marvin Lowenthal. There is only one complete translation in English, a five volume set edited by Raphael Patai and translated by Harry Zorn. Both the Lowenthal and Patai editions are quoted in this book.

10. *The Diaries of Theodor Herzl*, edited by Marvin Lowenthal, p. 18.

11. *The Diaries of Theodor Herzl*, edited by Marvin Lowenthal, p. 18.

12. *The Diaries of Theodor Herzl*, edited by Marvin Lowenthal, pp. 46–47.

13. *The Diaries of Theodor Herzl*, edited by Marvin Lowenthal, p. 3.

14. *The Complete Diaries of Theodor Herzl*, edited by Raphael Patai and translated by Harry Zohn (New York: Herzl Press, 1960), p. 219.

15. Theodor Herzl, *The Jewish State*, (Translated) (New York: American Zionist Emergency Council, 1946), p. 76.

16. *The Jewish State*, p. 72.

17. *The Jewish State*, p. 157.

18. *The Complete Diaries*, edited by Raphael Patai, p. 402.

19. *The Complete Diaries*, edited by Raphael Patai, p. 421.

20. *The Complete Diaries*, edited by Raphael Patai, p. 427.

21. *The Complete Diaries*, edited by Raphael Patai, p. 428.

22. *The Complete Diaries*, edited by Raphael Patai, p. 552.

23. *The Complete Diaries*, edited by Raphael Patai, pp. 578–579.

24. "Hatikvah" (Hope), originally the Zionist movement anthem, is now the national anthem of the State of Israel. It was written by the Hebrew poet, Naphtali Herz Imber (1856–1909) and set to a tune based on a traditional Rumanian folksong.

25. *The Complete Diaries*, edited by Raphael Patai, p. 581.

26. *The Complete Diaries*, edited by Raphael Patai, p. 733.

27. *The Complete Diaries*, edited by Raphael Patai, p. 734.

28. Rev. Z. H. Masliansky, "When Herzl Saw Palestine," *Theodor Herzl: A Memorial*, edited by Meyer W. Weisgal, p. 76.

This description is based on an interview with David Wolffsohn conducted by Rev. Masliansky.

29. *The Jewish Year Book*, 1899, edited by Cyrus Adler (Philadelphia: The Jewish Publication Society of America, 1899), p. 28.

Dr. Cyrus Adler (1863–1940) was an important American Jewish scholar. He served as President of the Jewish Theological Seminary of America and was editor of the American Jewish Year Book.

30. *The Complete Diaries*, edited by Raphael Patai, p. 1089.

31. *The Complete Diaries*, edited by Raphael Patai, p. 1473.

32. Psalm 137:5.

33. Arthur James Balfour (1848–1930) was a noted British statesman who, as Foreign Secretary, wrote an official letter to Lord Rothschild recognizing the right of the Jewish people to a homeland in Palestine. The Balfour Declaration became the basis for the establishment of the State of Israel in 1948. The original letter can be found in the British Museum in London.

34. *The Complete Diaries*, edited by Raphael Patai, p. 1603.

35. Rev. William Hechler, "The First Disciple," *Theodor Herzl: A Memorial*, edited by Meyer W. Weisgal, p. 52.

36. Psalm 137:5.

FOR FURTHER READING

Bein, Alex. *Theodor Herzl*. Translated by Maurice Samuel. New York: Atheneum, 1970.

Chouraqui, Andre. *A Man Alone*. Jerusalem: Keter, 1970.

Elon, Amos. *Herzl*. New York: Holt, Rinehart and Winston, 1975.

Herzl, Theodor. *The Complete Diaries of Theodor Herzl*. Edited by Raphael Patai and Translated by Harry Zohn. New York: Herzl Press, 1960. (5 Volumes)

Herzl, Theodor. *The Jewish State*. Translated by Harry Zohn. New York: Herzy Press, 1970.

Lowenthal, Marvin, ed. *The Diaries of Theodor Herzl*. New York: Dial Press, 1956. (Abridged)

Stewart, Desmond. *Theodor Herzl*. Garden City: Doubleday, 1974.

INDEX